TECHNOLOGY SERIES   Technical Memorandum No. 9

I0036052

Small-scale processing of pork

Prepared under the joint auspices of the International Labour Office and the United Nations Environment Programme

International Labour Office   Geneva

ISBN 92-2-100542-9
ISSN 0252-2004

First published 1985

PREFACE

This technical memorandum is the fourth in a series of publications dealing with food processing technologies[1]. The object of the series is to acquaint small-scale producers with alternative production techniques for specific products and processes with a view to helping them to choose and apply those techniques which are most appropriate to local socio-economic conditions.

A large number of developing countries raise pigs but continue to import large amounts of processed pig-meat in the form of sausages, bacon and ham. It is estimated that products worth over US$200 million are imported by developing countries each year, mostly from industrialised countries. Yet, developing countries are perfectly capable of processing their own pig-meat, thus saving scarce foreign exchange and generating much needed new employment opportunities. Furthermore, the local manufacture of pork products should better take into consideration local tastes and customs and the purchasing power of potential consumers of these products.

There are many reasons which may explain the large imports of pig-meat products by developing countries and the limited production of these products by local meat processors. Interested readers will find a brief analysis of these reasons in Chapter I. One such reason seems to be the lack of information on small-scale pig-meat processing technologies. It is hoped that this memorandum will help bridge this information gap and will induce the local processing of pig-meat in small-scale plants or as part of a butchery business.

---

[1] Published memoranda on food processing cover the following products: oil extraction from groundnuts and copra, small-scale processing of fish, small-scale maize milling and small-scale beef processing. Three other memoranda are at various stages of preparation: small-scale fruit processing, small-scale vegetable processing and small-scale grain storage.

This memorandum covers the production of six types of standard pig-meat products: fresh sausage, cooked sausage (e.g. mortadella), smoked cooked sausage (e.g. frankfurters), cooked ham (including comminuted ham), bacon and uncooked smoked sausage (e.g. Italian pork sausage, Thuringer, Polish sausage, tea sausage and Metwurst). Recipes and processing techniques are described in detail for the above types of pig-meat products. These may be easily adapted for the production of other local specialities not covered by this memorandum (e.g. through the addition of other ingredients or small variations in the various processing stages). Thus, with few exceptions, this memorandum should be of interest to the majority of pig-meat processors in developing countries.

The scale of production described in this memorandum does not exceed 2 tonnes of product per week. Production units with an output equal to or lower than 2 tonnes per week are defined as small-scale units. This is an arbitrary definition which does not take into consideration special circumstances under which pig-meat processing is carried out in various countries. Thus, units producing 2 tonnes of processed pig-meat per week may be considered medium-scale units in some countries and "micro units" in others. However, from a purely technological point of view (i.e taking into consideration available meat processing equipment), the upper limit for small-scale meat processing units is approximately 2 tonnes of product per week.

The processing techniques described in the memorandum are fairly simple and do not require automated or highly sophisticated equipment. However, most pieces of equipment are equipped with a small electric motor in view of the very low productivity of manually operated equipment. Unlike the other technical memoranda, no list of equipment suppliers is provided in this memorandum. The reason for this is that there is a very large number of meat processing equipment suppliers which are represented in most developing countries. Readers who may face difficulties locating equipment suppliers can obtain names and addresses from one of the directories or journals listed at the end of the memorandum.

Pig-meat processing may be operated as an entirely separate and independent business or may be an integral part of a slaughterhouse complex or of a butchery business. In general, circumstances (e.g. volume of demand for pig-meat products, location of production) will favour one or the other organisation of production. However, this technical memorandum focuses on the establishment of pig-meat processing units operating as separate businesses. This choice is made in order to facilitate the exposition of the various technical factors and requirements of pig-meat processing and to allow for a separate assessment of the viability of a projected plant. However, the information provided should allow, with some adaptations, the assessment of the technical and economic feasibility of processing units attached to a slaughterhouse or butchery business.

Two chapters of this memorandum (Chapters I and VI) are of particular interest to public planners, project evaluators from industrial development agencies and financial institutions. Chapter I analyses demand and supply of processed pig-meat in developing countries, including imports of pig-meat products and reasons for the limited supply of locally processed meat. Chapter VI evaluates the effects of alternative meat processing technologies on employment generation, foreign exchange savings, capital expenditures and rural industrialisation. A special section of this chapter is also devoted to the effects of alternative technologies on the environment, especially in relation to the disposal of wastes generated by small-scale and large-scale plants. These two chapters should help public planners to formulate policies and measures in favour of appropriate scales of production and meat processing technologies.

The remaining chapters (Chapters II to V) are of particular interest to small-scale meat processors. Chapter II describes the main raw materials (meat cuts, casings, spices, etc.) used in the manufacture of pig-meat products, while Chapter III describes the various pieces of equipment used in meat processing and provides some guide-lines for the design of a meat processing unit, including a suggested plant layout. Chapter IV describes in detail the techniques used for the production of the selected pig-meat products, including the recipe for a given batch of products and a description of the various processing stages. Finally, Chapter V suggests a methodological framework for the evaluation of alternative scales of production and processing technologies. This framework is applied to two production models for illustrative purposes.

A questionnaire is attached at the end of the memorandum for those readers who may wish to send the ILO their comments and suggestions on the content and usefulness of this publication. These will be taken into consideration in the preparation of future technical memoranda.

This technical memorandum was prepared by the Tropical Development and Research Institute (London) in collaboration with Mr. M. Allal, staff member in charge of the Technology Series within the Technology and Employment Branch of the ILO.

A. S. Bhalla,
Chief,
Technology and Employment Branch.

C O N T E N T S

APPENDICES

ACKNOWLEDGEMENTS

The publication of this technical memorandum has been made possible by a grant from the United Nations Environment Programme. The International Labour Office gratefully acknowledges this generous support.

Figures III.2, III.3, III.4, III.5, III.6, III.9: (c) British Crown Copyright, courtesy of TDRI.

CHAPTER I

SMALL-SCALE PORK PROCESSING IN DEVELOPING
COUNTRIES: SOME GENERAL CONSIDERATIONS

The purpose of this chapter is briefly to analyse demand, production and
trade of processed pork in developing countries, to identify the various types
of organisation of production in the pork processing sector, and to indicate
the scales of production, processing techniques and pork products covered by
this memorandum.

I. DEMAND, TRADE AND PRODUCTION

I.1 Imports of processed pig-meat by developing countries

Comprehensive information is not available on production and consumption
of traditional meat products in developing countries. However, trade
statistics indicate that steadily expanding markets for many kinds of meat
products exist in these countries. Total imports of processed meat by all
developing regions are substantial and rapidly growing (see table I.1). They
averaged 131,000 tonnes per annum for the period 1965-69 and 170,000 tonnes
per annum between 1970 and 1974, and exceeded 200,000 tonnes per annum by
1977. Total value of processed meat imports increased from an average of
US$106 million in 1965-69 to US$401 million in 1978, although an estimated 80
per cent of this increase is attributable to inflation.

Over the period shown in table I.1, annual imports of bacon and "bone-in"
ham have remained at approximately the same level, but imports of other meat
products have increased. Apart from bacon and "bone-in" ham it is difficult
to ascertain the animal derivation of the imports shown in the table.
However, estimates for the second half of the 1970s indicate that about 43

Table I.1

Imports of meat products by developing countries

(Average per annum)

Product	SITC (R2)	1965-69	1970-74	1975	1976	1977	1978
		(in thousands of tonnes)					
Canned or prepared meat	014.9	84	118	139	136	153	149
Bacon and ham	012.1	24	25	24	24	22	24
Sausages	014.2	14	17	17	17	20	22
Other dried salted smoked meat	012.9	9	10	12	16	14	12
Total		131	170	192	193	209	207
Total value (in million US\$ mainly c.i.f., 1984 prices)		106	183	295	311	370	401

Source: FAO Trade Yearbook (see Bibliography)

cent (by value) of total developing country imports of meat products are based on beef and 53 per cent on pig-meat, although these percentages may vary appreciably from year to year. The remainder (about 5 per cent) are based mainly on meat from sheep, goat, poultry and game. Thus, developing countries could have saved, in 1978, the equivalent of US$200 million in scarce foreign exchange had they processed their own pig-meat. Since most of these imports came from developed countries, the above gross savings would not have been made at the expense of other developing countries. In fact, actual net saving in foreign exchange to developing countries would have been lower than US$200 million (in 1978) because additional imports, mostly from developed countries (e.g. processing machinery, packaging materials, animal feed), would have been necessary for the local processing of pork. However, even though an accurate estimate cannot be made, significant net savings in foreign exchange could probably be achieved by some developing countries if processed pig-meat is produced locally instead of being imported.

I.2 Processing of pig-meat in developing countries

Despite the fact that some developing countries produce considerable numbers of livestock, meat processing plants have not developed on a large scale. A few exceptions to this situation mainly relate to large-scale canning operations. Major developments have been confined to the manufacture of beef rather than pig-meat products in some countries of South America and, to a lesser extent, of Africa. In the past, plants tended to be owned by foreign firms and production was primarily for export. This situation is changing in favour of local ownership. Most pig-meat is still produced and consumed locally in developing countries, either fresh or as distinctive products of traditional preservation processes.

However, the considerable volume of imports of processed pork by developing countries suggest that the latter could considerably expand production in order to satisfy local demand. What may, therefore, explain the lack of response from local meat processors? One explanation could be the characteristics of imported pork products. To a large extent, these are bland, mild cured products containing a low proportion of salt. They require high quality raw materials and are much more difficult to manufacture, store and distribute than traditional products since they are more susceptible to bacterial spoilage during processing and storage. An accurate control of cooking temperatures and times as well as the maintenance of an appropriate storage temperature are critical. High standards of hygiene at all stages of production and distribution are also essential. Thus, potential pig-meat processors in developing countries may have been reluctant to invest in projects requiring a level of expertise which is not available locally. Another explanation could be that sufficient supplies of pig-meat of the required quality may not have been forthcoming. Other factors may also have contributed to the lack of response to demand for processed beef: attempts at import substitution may have failed as a result of a retailer's bias against locally produced pork products; local producers may not have been sufficiently competitive vis-à-vis imports; or financial institutions may have been reluctant to provide credit for investments in this sector.

The above constraints, which slow down the expansion of pork processing in developing countries can be overcome if various measures are implemented in order to ensure sufficient supplies of good quality raw materials and the adoption of appropriate processing techniques by potential meat processors. Some of these techniques are described in this memorandum, including detailed information on a variety of processed pork products which are currently imported by a large number of developing countries.

II. ORGANISATION OF PRODUCTION

A pig-meat processing unit may be operated as an integral part of a slaughterhouse complex or of a butchery business, or as an entirely separate and independent enterprise. Market demand and circumstances determine the type of processing units which may be established in a country.

The integration of a pork processing unit into an existing slaughterhouse complex or butchery business offers a number of advantages. For example, a butcher may supply a segment of the local market with fresh or smoked sausage from edible meat trimmings. In this case, the value-added may be substantial while additional expenditures may be limited to a few raw materials (e.g. salt, spices, sausage casings) and low depreciation costs for the equipment (e.g. a hand-operated mincer). The extra labour may be provided by the butcher himself or a helper during idle periods. Similarly, the integration of a pork processing unit within a slaughterhouse may be advantageous in view of various economies of scale associated with this arrangement. These advantages do not mean that a pig-meat processing plant operating as an entirely separate business cannot be viable or be as competitive as the other types of plants. A sufficiently large scale of production and demand for specific pig-meat products may justify the establishment of a processing plant as an entirely separate business. Such plants operate profitably in a number of developing and developed countries and produce a large variety of pork products.

Although various approaches may be viable, this technical memorandum focuses on the establishment of pig-meat processing units operating as separate businesses. This choice is made in order to facilitate the exposition of the various technical factors and requirements of pig-meat processing and to allow a separate assessment of the viability of a projected plant. However, the information provided should allow, with some adaptation, the assessment of the technical and economic feasibility of processing units attached to a slaughterhouse or butchery business.

III. SCALE OF PRODUCTION, MEAT PROCESSING TECHNIQUES
     AND RANGE OF PRODUCTS

Meat processing technologies have greatly benefited from recent research and development in food preservation techniques, equipment design and computer-based automation. For example, some of the newly established large-scale plants are equipped with automated machines controlled from a computer room manned by highly skilled operators. Very few workers operate the machines or come into contact with the raw materials between the time these enter the plant and that at which they leave it as packaged meat products. Small-scale producers have also benefited from recent technical developments. For example, it is fairly common for a butchery business in a developed country to make use of meat grinders equipped with a temperature control system in order to avoid the overheating of meat during grinding.

The choice of scale of production is, to a large extent, a function of local and foreign market demand and the amount of pig-meat available for processing. Developing countries which produce large amounts of meat may establish large-scale meat processing plants if most of the production is geared for export. These plants must, of necessity, use capital-intensive technologies in view of the stringent quality control, product uniformity and high level of hygiene required by importers from industrialised countries. In many cases, the need for high technical performance and sophisticated marketing forces some developing countries to allow foreign investments or joint ventures whenever they wish to export processed meat products to industrialised countries.

While the establishment of large-scale, capital intensive plants may not be avoided whenever production is intented for export, small-scale, relatively labour-intensive units may be preferred if production is intended for the local market. In general, the limited demand for processed meat in developing countries, the high cost or lack of adequate transport facilities (e.g. road infrastructure, refrigerated trucks or wagons) and the limited supply of pig-meat within a given area point in favour of the establishment of such small-scale units. Furthermore, the latter contribute to important development objectives such as employment generation and the improvement of the balance of payments (see chapter VI). For these reasons, and given the main purpose of the technical memoranda series, this memorandum provides detailed technical and economic information on small-scale pig-meat processing only. Readers interested in large-sale meat processing plants should obtain information from equipment manufacturers or engineering firms since the establishment of these plants require very detailed proprietary information which is outside the scope of this technical memorandum.

The scale of production described in the following chapters is limited to a few tonnes of pork products per week. Two plants with outputs of one to two tonnes per week are discussed in detail and are used as illustrative examples for the estimation of unit production costs (see Chapter V).

The processing techniques described in Chapter III are relatively simple but do, nevertheless, require electrically-powered equipment which is seldom manufactured in developing countries. In some cases, lower-cost manually-operated equipment may also be adequate. However, the productivity of some of the equipment is so low that it may be more profitable to use the more expensive electrically-powered equipment. Potential meat processors need to assess the alternative pieces of equipment as described in Chapter V in order to identify those which minimise unit production costs. This assessment takes into consideration equipment and labour productivity, the prevailing wage level, the unit cost of electric power and the acquisition cost of the alternative pieces of equipment.

The range of pig-meat products covered by this memorandum includes the following:

- fresh uncooked sausage;
- uncooked smoked sausage (e.g. Metwurst);
- cooked sausage (e.g. mortadella);
- smoked cooked sausage (e.g. frankfurters);
- cooked ham; and
- bacon.

Production of fresh, chilled or frozen pig-meat is not covered. Similarly, manufacture of canned pig-meat products is not included since small-scale canning plants are unlikely to be financially viable.

The techniques described for the six pig-meat products listed above may be adapted for the production of local specialties which have similar characteristics (i.e. different ingredients may be used or some of the subprocesses may be slightly altered). Thus, information contained in this memorandum could be useful for the production of a fairly large range of pork products.

CHAPTER II

RAW MATERIALS

Meat used in the manufacture of processed pork products includes cuts and trimmings from various locations in the carcase. This chapter provides information on the sources and subsequent selection of meat used in pork products, and describes other ingredients required by these products.

I. SOURCE AND SELECTION OF CARCASE MEAT

Pig-meat is not a uniform commodity. It may be derived from pigs of different breeds, sexes and ages. Its composition and quality may vary according to the type of feed used and the way the animal is handled prior to and at the point of slaughter.

Many breeds of pigs are found in the tropics, both indigenous and genetically improved, imported breeds. Some of the so-called lard pigs of Latin America and the Far East are early maturing varieties that carry a substantial amount of carcase and body fat at slaughter weight. This can substantially reduce lean meat yield and limit the use of these pigs for pork processing operations. The introduction of exotic breeds for cross-breeding in order to improve carcase characteristics and increase production has, however, resulted in the loss of some valuable traits in the indigenous breeds (e.g. fertility, and mothering ability).

In the tropics as elsewhere, pigs are slaughtered at a wide range of body weights. The early-maturing breeds tend to have more fat - at the same live weight - than breeds which are late maturing. However, irrespective of breed, the relative amounts of lean meat, fat and bone change as a pig grows (see table II.1). In many countries, the measurement of fat depth at specified points along the loin of a freshly slaughtered animal allows a purchaser to choose his carcase according to levels of fatness, and therefore to anticipate lean meat yield. In most developing countries, however, where such differentiation at source does not occur, a manufacturer must use experience and a trained eye to choose suitable high yielding carcases. Profitability will depend very heavily on the maximum possible utilisation of the carcase for the range of products to be manufactured. A processor must be aware of the differences in cut-out yield and should also be discerning in the choice of pigs he needs for his own particular processing operation.

Table II.1
Body composition as affected by live-weight
(Danish Landrace Breed)

Live-weight (kg)	Dressing out (%)	Dressed carcase composition (less head) Percentage of		
		Fat	Lean meat	Bone
20	70.0	23.7	57.5	18.8
50	73.2	30.8	54.5	14.7
90	76.9	37.0	51.1	11.9
120	79.0	40.6	48.6	10.8

Very heavy old pigs with excessive fat levels are generally unsuitable for pork processing unless they can be purchased at fairly low prices. Very young lean pork carcases, on the other hand, are unsuitable for the production of bacon since moderate fat levels are necessary for product appearance and palatability.

II. SLAUGHTER AND CARCASE HANDLING

Careful control of the slaughter operation is essential for the production of good quality pork products. Although a manufacturer will generally be unable to ensure that he is supplied from well managed and hygienic abattoirs, careful examination of the carcase will offer clues as to its likely quality.

Carcases smeared with blood, faecal material or dirt should not be used for the manufacture of pork products. Only clean, undamaged carcases free of all offal, apart from the kidney, should be purchased. A manufacturer should also look for marks indicating that the animal has been inspected by a qualified veterinarian.

All meat for onward processing must be certified as free from infectious diseases if any of the products are to be sold uncooked or partially cooked (i.e. when their internal temperature does not reach 60°C).

Pigs that are highly stressed before slaughter may produce carcase meat that is pale in colour and soft and watery in appearance (exudative). Pale, soft and watery meat loses weight rapidly during cooking and smoking with a resultant decrease in processing yields. The binding property of the meat is also impaired, thus seriously affecting products requiring the production of an emulsion during processing (e.g. frankfurters).

Abnormally dark meat also occurs occasionally in animals badly handled prior to slaughter or exhausted after long road journeys. Dark meat has a sticky texture and water loss during cooking and curing is greatly reduced. Although dark meat is thought to produce more tender products, it does restrict salt penetration and hence promotes microbial growth.

Both PSE (pale, soft, exudative) and DFD (dark, firm and dry) pork should be avoided. It is, however, often difficult to detect these two conditions in the intact carcase. The muscle most affected by variations in colour caused by bad handling is the loin. A processor who uses carcases for either the fresh or processed meat trade is advised to make an initial cut through the loin for selection purposes.

Whole carcases should be chilled at the abattoir to an internal temperature not exceeding 7°C, except in the case where pre-rigor pork is used[1]. When a delivery is suspected of containing carcases that have not been properly refrigerated, the processor should carefully examine the carcase for signs of taint caused by bacterial spoilage. By cutting into the leg muscle overlying the pelvis, it should be possible to detect by smell any deterioration caused by growth of bacteria. Chilled carcases that are wet or slimy should also be avoided, since this is indicative of poor handling and ineffective refrigeration.

III. CHOICE OF CUTS FOR PORK PROCESSING

Trade and economic circumstances influence the supply of meat for the manufacture of processed meat products. In small-scale production by retail butchers, the meat is usually derived from the cheaper parts of the carcase or from trimmings produced by the dressing and cutting of pork. Market requirements generally dictate the nature of the cuts and the quantity of trimmings. Only as a business expands is meat purchased specifically for processing. Many large-scale operators which have no other outlets for the meat process all that they purchase. Processors of pig-meat in the tropics frequently buy live pigs which they slaughter themselves. They often sell cuts of fresh meat taken from the carcase.

III.1 Meat cuts

The various types of cuts used in pig-meat processing are briefly described below:

Primal cuts

Certain whole primal cuts may be removed from the pig carcase for processing. The following brief description of primal butchery is given for the benefit of trained butchers to enable them to identify the primal cuts used in subsequent processing operations. Training in butchery techniques is needed before attempting primal cutting.

Usually, the carcase is first split into sides by dividing down the centre of the back to the point of the skull. The left side is then cut free of the head by a cut close to the ear and the back edge of the jaw bone. The head is removed by repeating the cut on the right side of the carcase and manoeuvring the knife between the skull and the first cervical vertebra.

---

[1] Hot-boned or pre-rigor pork is material which has not undergone refrigeration as a whole carcase but is instead butchered directly after slaughter for onward, immediate processing. The slaughter and processing facilities must be adjacent and kept very clean since introduced micro-organisms multiply rapidly during a hot-meat handling operation.

Figure II.1 illustrates primal cuts and main muscle components of pig carcases.

Cheek meat

Pork cheeks and head meat are removed from the intact skull after careful separation of the cheek fat. This fat is often used for sausage manufacture but particular attention must be given to complete removal of any glandular tissue and blood left after sticking. Cheek meat is mainly used for making sausage.

The leg

The leg is removed by cutting with a knife about 1 cm below the anterior edge of the aitchbone to a point immediately in front of the tail and continuing across in a straight line through the flank. The bone is cut through with a pork saw. The leg is generally used for the production of ham.

The hand and belly

The hand and belly are usually removed together from the carcase by sawing through the ribs along the line shown in figure II.1. The cut is extended between the joint in the foreleg with a boning knife. Depending upon local butchery practice, the belly and flank regions are then separated from the hand. This is usually carried out by cutting between the first and second ribs. The hand is mainly used in second grade ham products and processed sausage.

The meat of the flank and belly is thin, and, if separated from the underlying fat, can be used in comminuted products.

The loin

The loin is normally separated from the neck region between the fourth and fifth ribs. The muscle must be removed carefully from the backbone with a small boning knife. Loin can be incorporated into comminuted ham products or sausage.

The blade and neck

Using a long knife, the blade of the shoulder is removed from the underlying muscle. The remainder neck cut must be carefully deboned to avoid the removal of cartilage and bone with the meat. Excess fat and all rind and glandular material should be removed. The muscle of the blade region should be trimmed of excess fat and blood vessels. The blade and neck are generally

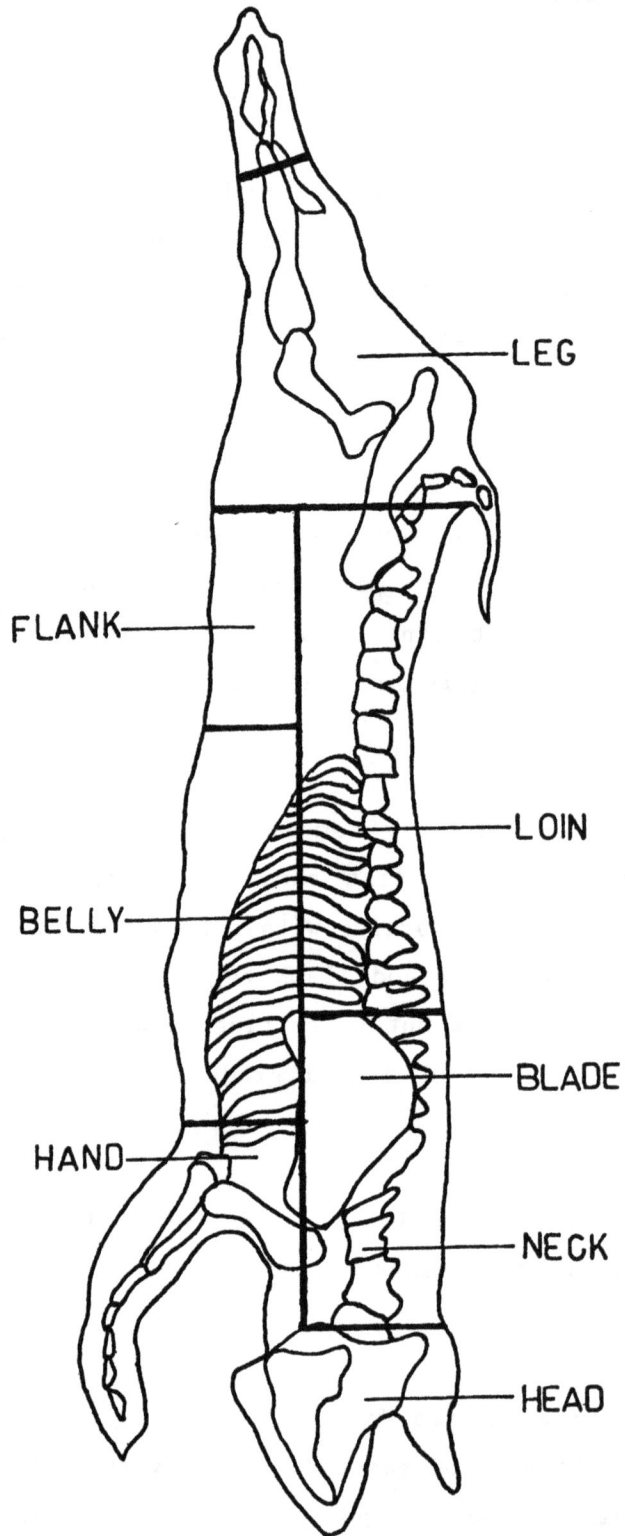

Figure II.1

Pig carcase showing primal cuts with major muscle components

Pork trimmings

Trimmings from the fresh meat trade are usually classified according to the ratio of fat to lean meat. Lean pork trimmings, containing between 10 and 30 per cent fat, are selected for use in products such as Mortadella, uncooked smoked sausages and good-quality frankfurters. Regular pork trimmings may contain up to 60 per cent fat and are usually mixed with lean trimmings or selected cuts for fresh sausage manufacture or use in some of the cooked sausages. Particular care must be taken in handling the trimmings to keep them in a fresh condition.

Trimmings originating from the associated cutting area can be segregated during primal butchery and visually assessed for grade. "Bought-in" trimmings of unknown origin should be sample dissected and weighed into component protein and fat. The exact analysis of trimmings will require laboratory techniques. These are only necessary in cases of high throughputs and diverse product range.

Bacon cuttings

The preparation of sides of pork for the manufacture of bacon is outlined in Chapter IV under processing procedures.

III.2 Storage and selection of meat ingredients

Carcase meat, cuts or trimmings should be used immediately or within 24 hours of delivery if held in the chilled state at 0-2°C. Extra care in handling pork trimmings is necessary. In particular, it is important to maintain their low temperature state by quick transfer to the chill store. Trimmings which are not for immediate use should be held in a cold store at -10°C or a lower temperature. They should be compacted and wrapped in air-tight polythene bags to prevent the fat from becoming rancid and the meat from losing its colour.

The proper selection of meat ingredients is essential for the production of processed pork products of uniform quality. Recognised standards of the gross raw materials with respect to lean/fat ratios and microbiological conditions should be known and consistently met. Additionally, different tissues vary in their moisture to protein ratios, their lean to fat ratios, the relative amounts of pigment they contain, and their water-binding properties. All of these properties will affect the characteristics of the end-product.

For instance, head meat, cheek meat, most primal cuts and lean trimmings have medium to high binding properties. Regular trimmings and very fatty tissues, on the other hand, have low binding properties. Thus, whilst regular trimmings may be nutritionally acceptable, they may not constitute a large fraction of the processed meat if the overall quality of the end product is to be maintained.

Variations in the price of certain materials will necessitate flexibility in product formulations. While the small producer may need to keep these to a minimum, large producers may substitute raw materials in times of shortage or in order to increase their profit margins, because they are capable of investigating the effect of these substitutions on the quality of the end product. Small producers must rely on experience to determine the formulations and quality standards which maximise their profit margins.

IV. NON-MEAT INGREDIENTS

A number of non-meat ingredients are used in pig-meat processing. These are briefly described below.

Ice in meat products

Moisture, added as ice at the time of chopping, is important in the formulation and preparation of smoked and fresh pork products. Many of these products would be dry and unpalatable if they contained only the moisture inherent in the meat ingredients. Ice is also necessary to hold the temperature of the emulsion below that which would make it unstable, and to produce appropriate brine strengths for maximum binding of the meat proteins. Where ice is to be incorporated directly into a product, it is added either in the flake or crushed form.

Salt

Salt is a critical ingredient in sausage manufacture. Apart from its role as a preservative, and in the preparation of meat emulsions, it is important in imparting recognisable product flavour. Levels higher than 3.0-3.5 per cent in the finished meat product are said to produce an undesirable 'salty' taste. However, since salt tolerance is known to vary, only a consumer test can determine the salt levels best suited to the local market tastes.

Impurities in the salt can cause rancidity in the final product. Thus, heavily contaminated or dirty salt should be avoided. A high moisture content lowers the effective amount of salt present in a given product weight. Spoilage of the product will occur if this is not taken into account whenever salt is the main preservation ingredient. Storage of salt in sealed containers is therefore recommended.

Nitrates and nitrites

Nitrates (as Salpetre-Potassium Nitrate or Chilli Salpetre Sodium Nitrate) and nitrites (as Potassium or Sodium Nitrite) are added to curing ingredients in order to develop the characteristic red or pink colour in the cured meat. In addition, nitrites perform other critical functions. They affect flavour directly or through their action as powerful anti-oxidants that prevent the development of rancidity. Sodium nitrite is also an effective inhibitor of the growth of certain dangerous food poisoning bacteria.[1]

Nitrate is not directly involved in the curing reaction: it is converted to nitrite by a slow process which depends upon the presence of bacteria in the brine and in the meat. Thus, nitrite alone is often used in many rapidly processed products.

The role of nitrates and nitrites in meat curing is currently under review. Nitrites have been implicated in the formation of potentially harmful nitrosamines in bacon and strict limits on their use have been established in many countries. Levels in excess of 200 parts per million (ppm) of sodium nitrate and 100 ppm of sodium nitrite should not be used.

Nitrate and nitrite are added in small amounts. They may be directly dissolved in water if used with brines. For dry cures, they may be initially dispersed in the salt component to ensure uniform distribution. Nitrite salt, used for rapidly produced products, consists of 99.5 per cent salt and 0.5 per cent sodium nitrite. It is made up on a daily basis.

Sugars

Sugars, such as sucrose and dextrose, are used in the manufacture of sausages to improve product flavour and colour, mask saltiness and in some cases, to bring about necessary chemical and microbial changes in the product.

---

[1] Sodium nitrite is added to inhibit the growth of Clostridium botulinum, a food poisoning organism which produces a fatal toxin.

The levels of sugar added are limited by regulation in some countries. Amounts in excess of 2.5 per cent by product weight are not recommended. Artificial sweeteners, such as saccharine, are used in some countries at a level of 0.01 per cent to improve the flavour of bacon.

Extenders

A number of products, such as non-fat dried skimmed milk, cereal flours and soya protein are used to raise the level of protein in sausages. In general, these are added to the lower quality products for economic reasons although some do improve binding qualities, cooking yields and slicing characteristics. It is thought that other extenders improve flavour by their sweetening effect. Allowable amounts are often regulated and depend upon the type of product to be processed. However, non-meat protein additions in excess of 10 per cent do result in uncharacteristic textures and flavours.

Spices and seasonings

Spices, aromatic substances of vegetable origin, herbs (e.g. leaves of sage) and vegetables (e.g. garlic and onions) are used to season pork products.

Spices may be added as a natural spice or as spice extract. The extracts are easier to store because they are less bulky than the natural product. Most spices contain moulds and bacteria which can cause considerable damage to products under conditions favourable to their growth. Some spice manufacturers sell 'purified spices' where the level of contamination is greatly reduced. However, the purification processes are not totally efficient and some risk remains in their use.

Spices, herbs and vegetables should be stored in a dry goods store, preferably in sealed containers. They should not be exposed to direct sunlight or steam and should only be ground or crushed on the day of manufacture.

A list of some of the seasonings used in processing is given in table II.2.

Sausage casings

There are two main types of casings used in the manufacture of processed pork products: animal casings (also called natural casings) made from the stomach, intestines and bladders of cattle, hogs and sheep, and synthetic or manufactured casings which may be made from cellulose or collagen and which

Table II.2

Common seasonings used in pork products

Description	Uses
A. Spices	
Allspice (pimento)	Used in a variety of sausages, including pork sausage and pickled pigs'feet
Cayenne pepper	Used as a partial replacement for black pepper in frankfurters and some smoked sausages
Cinnamon	Astringent and sweet, used in some countries in Mortadella and Bologna sausage
Clove	Whole cloves stuck into hams when they are cooked
Ginger	Used in frankfurters and fresh pork sausages
Mace	Used to flavour fresh pork sausages and frankfurters
Nutmeg	Used in minced ham sausages
Paprika	Mild pepper and colouring agent used in frankfurters and some minced products
Black/white pepper	Used in a variety of pork products. White pepper should be used where a light product colour is required
B. Aromatic seeds	
Cardamon seeds	Rapid loss of aromatic constituents during storage. Limited use
Celery seed	Principally used in fresh pork sausage
Coriander seed	Contains fatty matter and tannins. May be used in frankfurters, minced ham, Polish sausage and pork luncheon meat
Cumin seed	Used principally in the manufacture of curry powder
Anis seed	May be used in dry sausage and Mortadella
C. Herbs	
Bay leaves	Used for the pickling of pigs'feet and pork tongue
Marjoram	Used in Polish sausage
Sage	Used in pork sausage and baked pork loaf
Thyme	Used in pork sausage and Bockwurst
D. Condimental vegetables	
Garlic	Used in Polish sausage and some smoked sausages
Onion	Often used to replace garlic

are either edible or non-edible. The processing of animal casings is labour-intensive and involves a considerable amount of cleaning and stripping away of unwanted layers. It should not be carried out by untrained personnel.

(i)   Natural casings : In the production of casings, high yield and good quality depend upon the complete removal of fat, nerves, blood and lymphatic vessels without damaging the remaining tissues. The intestines are removed without puncturing and their gross fat is trimmed off. They are then detached from the mesenteric tissue into strands (termed "running"), and cut into appropriate lengths and types. The contents of the intestines are removed by stripping either by machine or by hand, under warm water, by easing through a restricted aperture in the case of small casings and by turning them inside out and massaging with large casings. Small casings are then "slimed" by repeated passing through rollers and strippers or by hand working after a prolonged soaking in lukewarm water (one to six hours depending upon source) in order to remove the mucosa and muscle layers. Large casings are passed through crushing rollers inside out and brushed (rice root and bristle) under a hot spray. Hand treatment is by careful brushing under warm water.

Washed casings are stored overnight in cold, 20 per cent saturated salt solution. Their quality is checked by inflation and visual inspection for scars and perforations. They are subsequently rubbed with medium dry salt and left for one week to cure. Excess coarse salt is then removed and fine salt is rubbed in. They are finally packed (usually in a 55 gallon barrel or a tierce) and held at 5°C until use. It is usual for the user to recheck the quality on immediate arrival from the supplier. The variety and uses of animal casings are shown in table II.3.

Natural casings are generally received by the pork processor in lengths of 80 to 100 metres, either dried or salted. Ideally, they should be stored at 5°C. At any rate, they must never be frozen or exposed to heat. If allowed to absorb water, they will spoil and become worthless. Casings stored dry at 5°C can keep for several weeks. If possible, casings should be used the same day they are removed from salt. Any left-over casings must be re-salted even if they are for use the following day.

(ii) Manufactured casings: The use of manufactured casings has increased significantly in recent years as a result of demand for uniformity of stuffed diameter, ease of handling and high resilience to

Table II.3

Animal casings and their use

Variety	Description	Uses
Small hog casings	Narrow, medium and wide gauges of small intestine	Fresh sausage, Polish sausage and frankfurters
Hog bungs	Straight, large intestine	Dry sausage, liver sausage
Hog middles	Appendix vermiformis	Italian type sausages
Hog stomach	Stomach	Mortadella sausage
Sheep casings or "strings"	Small and large intestine graded according to un-stuffed diameters	Used for top quality frankfurters and fresh sausage
Beef rounds	Small intestine	Metwurst, Bologna sausage
Beef middles	Large intestine	Many "continental-type" sausages
Beef weasands	Oesophagus from throat to first stomach	Bologna and salami sausage, luncheon meats
Beef bungs	Appendix vermiformis	Large cooked sausages
Beef bladders	Bladder	Mortadella and French garlic sausage.

Cellulose casings, produced from cotton, may be grouped into three types:

(a) <u>Small cellulose casings</u> are used for the manufacture of skinless frankfurters, skinless fresh pork sausages and similar kinds of small sized pork products. They may be purchased either clear or coloured, in lengths ranging from 25 to 55 metres.

(b) <u>Large cellulose casings</u> are available in three types: regular, high-stretch and light-weight casings. Large regular casings are used for many types of processed pork products and act primarily as a container. High stretch casings are specially treated to give the casing extra stretch and shrink characteristics. They are particularly useful for the manufacture of cubed ham products where meat adhesion is a desirable characteristic. Light-weight casings, which have very thin walls, are suitable for any smoked meats such as ham.

(c) <u>Fibrous casings</u> have high strength characteristics and are used in cases where a maximum uniformity of finished product diameter is desired. They are therefore ideal for products which must be sliced into pre-packaged commodities. Several types of fibrous casings are available, differing in their treatment and the uses to which they are put. Moisture impermeable fibrous casings are used to improve the keeping quality of certain products, but they are also impermeable to smoke: they should only be used for water-cooked items such as liver sausage. Special fibrous casings which adhere to the meat contents during dehydration and shrinkage are also available. These are particularly useful in the manufacture of dried products such as salami. For the manufacture of dry sausage products (e.g. salami), it is recommended that the casings be dipped in a 2.5 per cent solution of potassium sorbate (EEC Additive No. E202) in order to inhibit mould growth.

II.8 Colourants

Spices of the capsicum family (e.g. paprika, chillies and various peppers) are used as colouring aids as well as to improve product flavour. Paprika is high in colour and low in flavour, while red pepper is high in both pungency and colour. Extracted resins from these spices may be used instead of the ground natural forms. Other natural colouring agents used in sausage manufacture include annatto, carotene, cochineal, saffron and turmeric.

Certain artificial colouring agents, which have been approved by the relevant authorities, may also be used in levels sufficient for the purpose. These are usually mixed with approved natural colouring ingredients in harmless inert materials such as salt or sugar.

Flavouring enhancers

A number of natural products are used as flavouring agents in sausage production. Harmless bacterial starters, such as lactic acid starter, are used to develop flavour in dry sausage, pork roll, Thuringer, Bologna and salami sausage. These may be included at the 0.5 per cent level.

Monosodium glutamate is also frequently used in ham products in order to improve flavour. A full list of additives used in the manufacture of processed meats, including permitted levels of use, is given in Appendix I.

CHAPTER III

SMALL-SCALE PLANT AND FACILITIES

The type and extent of plant and machinery necessary for the manufacture of pork products depend upon the size of the proposed operation and the variety of products to be processed. Before entering the processed meat trade, the processor must decide what range and quantity of products he is going to manufacture, bearing in mind his estimates of demand and of the available resources (capital, raw materials, and so on).

The processor must seek to add high value to his processed commodity. On very small throughputs, this often means specialising in a single product from a particular raw material component in addition to the sale of fresh meat. Therefore, very small-scale production is often associated with a small retail butchery business.

For illustrative purposes, this memorandum considers principles of plant operation, buildings and equipment needed for two small-scale units producing a small selection of products (see Chapter IV). Both units utilise whole carcases, but certain cuts are diverted to different purposes to allow for demand pattern differences. These two units (designated as Model 1 and Model 2) are only examples of possible product mixes. They do not represent recommendations as to the most appropriate production quantity or mix which must be adopted by a small-scale unit. These can only be determined in the light of specific local market situations. These model operations (summarised in table III.1) are used in Chapter V to calculate fixed capital and annual operating costs.

Table III.1

Weekly production profiles for Model 1 and Model 2

Product	Raw material source	Processing	Amount (kg) per week
Model 1			
Ham	Leg, hand (part)	Cured, deboned, cooked	500
Mortadella	Loin, blade, belly, lean trimmings	Chopped, cased, cooked	1 200
Fresh sausage	Neck, flank, head, regular trimmings	Minced, cased, fresh	300
Total			2 000
Model 2			
Ham	Leg, hand, blade	Cured, deboned, shaped, cooked	640
Comminuted ham	Loin, belly, flank (part), lean trimmings	Deboned, cured, tumble formed, cooked	720
Fresh sausage	Neck, head, regular trimmings	Minced, cased, fresh	240
Total			1 600

I. PLANT LAYOUT

Although a plant layout depends to a large extent, upon building shape and floor area, the simplified layout suggested in figure III.1 embodies principles of construction and design that should be followed as far as possible whatever the other limitations might be.

The movement of product should try to follow an unbroken path from the receipt of the raw materials and the holding chill room where it is stored, through the various preparation and processing operations, to the area of dispatch.

In large units, conditions of hygiene require the physical separation of areas set aside for pork sausage and cured meat product processing. This is not possible in very small plants of limited space. In this case, every effort should be made to ensure that fresh meat and processed meat are not being handled concurrently.

In the scheme set out in figure III.1, carcase meat is delivered at point A where it is weighed and inspected before being placed in the 0°C holding room. All butchery operations and fresh sausage manufacture should be carried out on tables situated in area B, while all cured product operations should be handled on tables located in the separate area C.

Ideally, all processing operations should be carried out under refrigeration. However, this requires very large capital investments which cannot be justified for small-scale operations. The plant embodies a series of centrally placed chill rooms which also act as a physical barrier between the fresh and cured meat processing areas. Chill room temperatures should be variable in order to deal with specific processing requirements.

All cooking and smoking operations should be carried out in a separate room to facilitate the control of steam and waste-water disposal and to prevent the temperature from rising in the processing area.

I.1 Raw material storage and refrigerated curing rooms

The design and operation of cold storage facilities require professional expertise, especially in tropical environments where problems associated with the extraction of heat in high ambient temperatures are compounded by condensation from high humidity levels. The advice of a local expert must be sought at the project evaluation stage.

Raw materials, in the form of entire carcases or pork trimmings, should be stored in a walk-in cold store (holding room) operating between 0°C and 4°C. The store should be located as close as possible to the reception area, and all deliveries should be carefully examined, weighed and date-coded. Calculation of the size of store depends upon the delivery of raw materials and production sequence. For small-scale units, deliveries are usually made on a daily basis.

Carcases must hang in a way which allows sufficient space between them for personnel to move around. The calculation of hanging room dimensions for the two models under consideration takes account of the following carcase and rail

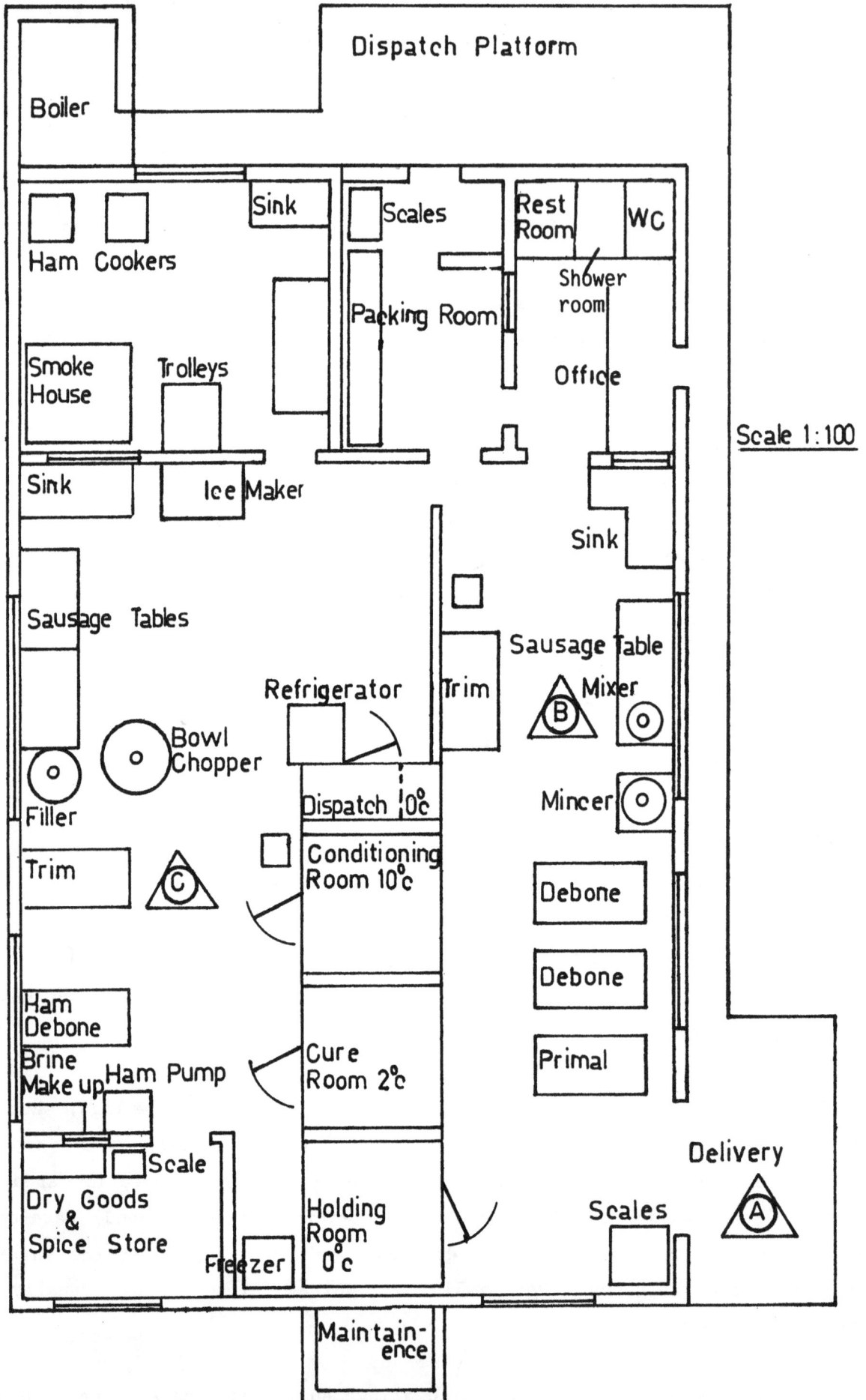

Figure III.1

A schematic floor plan for a small-scale pork processing plant

| | Distance between rails (metres) | | Minimum distance between |
	Minimum	Desirable	carcases along rails (metres)
Beef	0.9	0.9	0.20
Pigs	0.46	0.7	0.20
Lamb	0.46	0.46	0.15

There should be a gap of at least 20 cm between carcase surfaces and a walking space between cold-store walls and carcase meat to facilitate movement. For very small cold stores, the area per carcase is estimated at $0.48 \ m^2$. Taking into account a movement factor of 1.4, actual area per carcase is equal to $0.67 \ m^2$ (i.e. 1.4 x 0.48).

The above factors may be used to calculate the raw material cold store area for Model 1 as follows:

- carcase meat demand (bone-in): 450 kg/day (estimates based on
  recipes for ham, mortadella and fresh sausage provided in Chapter IV);
- average weight per carcase: 50 kg;
- no. of carcases required: 9;
- cold store area : $9 \ x \ 0.67m^2 = 6.03 \ m^2$

This area is shown in figure III.1 as a cold store area of $6.25 \ m^2$ (2.5 x 2.5 m) in order to allow for the storage of trimmings from the previous day.

The raw material cold store should have an operating temperature of $2°C$ with a tolerance of $+ \ 2°C$. The relative humidity should be maintained between 85 and 90 per cent.

Cured meat products are more stable than fresh meats but tend, at elevated temperatures, to undergo deteriorative chemical changes which spoil their taste. They should thus be kept chilled during and after processing, the degree of refrigeration depending upon the type of product. Chapter IV gives the temperature at which particular products should be maintained. Since most processing operations produce a variety of products, a degree of flexibility is needed in the curing rooms regarding temperature control.

The dimensions of curing rooms are difficult to calculate in view of the variety of products that they might contain consecutively or concurrently.

The volume occupied by the product must first be calculated, remembering that it will change during the overall operation. For example, an estimation of the volumes of the maturation room and the curing room for ham processing must take into consideration the fact that the volume of meat to be matured is 1.33 times that of the end-product (since meat is matured with the bones still in), and that the addition of brine for curing requires that the curing room be three times the size of the maturing room.

Appendix II provides estimates of the factors used in the determination of the volume of the curing and maturation rooms required for the products described in Chapter IV. Total area occupied by a variety of products also depends on product distribution within the cold store. For instance, ham curing in 300 litre containers occupies a single layer (the ground space) for ease of handling while other products may be stacked above.

Specialist advice should be sought regarding refrigerative capacity, the determination of which depends on a variety of factors within the cold store as well as climatic conditions. Information on size, product flow and cold store distribution will need to be collected for the estimation of cold store volumes by a refrigeration engineer.

I.2 Finished products stores

All finished, cured products should be held under refrigeration prior to dispatch. They should be kept separate from all unprocessed raw materials. Care should be taken to ensure that they are properly packaged and date-coded. The size of the store depends upon the system of marketing employed. It should, however, be sufficient to obviate dispatch difficulties. The size of stores should be calculated on the basis of product occupancy volume, marketing procedures and a movement allowance of 1.5.

Uncured, fresh pork sausage should be stored in a separate or partitioned cold store at 0°C prior to dispatch.

I.3 Dry goods store

A room for the storage of spices and processing ingredients not requiring refrigeration, for processing equipment and for packaging materials should be included in the plant layout. The size of the room is directly related to the number of products processed and, more important, to the frequency of delivery of these specialist items. It must be remembered that spices and colourants tend to lose their properties with age, and that the storage period should, therefore, be as short as possible.

This room may also be used as a weighing area for curing ingredients and spices.

I.4 Cooking and smoking room

The cooking room, which should be of generous dimensions and separated from the main processing area by self-closing doors, should contain all the equipment used in the cooking and smoking of the products. It must be well ventilated to ensure the exit of steam and smoke, have adequate drainage and be served with treated cooling water. The steam boiler (and generator/compressor) may be located in a separate building close to but separate from this area.

I.5 Main processing hall

The layout of the main processing hall should facilitate uninterrupted product movement and eliminate the need for excessive product handling. Table-mounted mincers, mixers and stuffers should be sufficient to cope with the limited throughputs of small-scale units. The tables should be of stainless steel. Carcase butchering should be carried out on high density polythene cutting blocks instead of traditional wooden blocks which are less hygienic and more difficult to keep clean.

The size of the processing hall may be estimated on the basis of the area occupied by the various pieces of equipment and of an assumed access circumference of 0.5 m multiplied by a movement allowance of 1.4. This estimation procedure applies, in particular, to small-scale meat processing plants. Large units (e.g. 5 tonnes per day) utilising large pieces of equipment, tend to have a greater product movement area (e.g. a movement allowance factor of 2) in order to promote the maximum efficiency of labour.

The processing room should be constructed in materials that may be easily cleaned and yet provide a safe and pleasant working environment. Particular care must be given to lighting, drainage and service facilities and to the provision of a non-slip floor.

II. PROCESSING EQUIPMENT

A minimum list of meat processing equipment should include simple equipment for the mincing and mixing of meat components and that needed to smoke and cook the finished product. Equal importance must be given to the range of tables, trucks, scales, bins and other accessories necessary for a fluent operation. Having decided the range and quantities of products required, the processor must choose among alternative processing techniques. The cost and quality of local labour may influence the system chosen. In particular, the processor may have the option of choosing either a labour-intensive system utilising less sophisticated equipment or a capital-intensive system involving larger initial investments but lower labour costs.

Appendix III provides estimates of the productivity of labour and of various pieces of equipment for the main meat processing operations (e.g. mincing, mixing, stuffing). These estimates may be used to determine the size and number of pieces of equipment required for a given scale of production, taking into consideration the number of shifts per day and the number of working hours per shift, as well as the sequence and duration of processing stages. Some pieces of equipment (e.g. mincers) will be used full time while others will only be used part of the time. Consequently, the capacity or rate of the former pieces of equipment will determine the scale of production.

In units producing a variety of products, flexibility is necessary to meet demand changes in particular products. Equipment installed for operation by a single worker should be operable by more labour in times of increased demand. For instance, installed equipment for a 5.15 kg batch of meat products may have an operating daily throughput of 45 kg for single-worker man operation and 235 kg for four workers (although this does not include additional tables, and so on). If sausage is only one of a variety of products, equipment output can be varied considerably by mobility of labour within the unit. Thus, for Model 1 (for which installed equipment corresponds to a 20.6 kg batch capacity), the entire unit output could be transferred to fresh sausage production by reallocation of labour.

Equipment for use in the tropics must have the following characteristics: to be made of appropriate materials to avoid corrosion; rugged construction to minimise maintenance; satisfactory design to limit the handling of meat and to facilitate thorough cleaning after use; and the capacity to meet any expected production requirements. All equipment should be provided with the necessary safeguards to ensure that it is not hazardous to operators. The most important pieces of equipment of interest to small-scale meat processing units are briefly described below.

II.1 Mincers

Mincers are used to cut meat into small pieces so that they may be thoroughly mixed with other ingredients or curing salts. During mincing, meat is fed from the hopper to the mincing plate by means of an auger. As the meat is extruded through the holes in the plate, it is sliced by revolving knives. Plates with holes of various sizes are available, depending upon whether the meat is to be cut into large or small pieces. In general, plates with perforations varying between 3 mm and 8 mm are used for sausage manufacture. Unless mincer plates and knives are kept in good condition, meat will be heated during mincing and will lose quality. Power costs will also be increased and delays experienced in passing material through the mincer.

Hand mincers are available in capacities up to 50 kg/hour. However, all hand mincers require that the raw material be previously reduced to portions of approximately 100 mm by 50 mm. In addition to their higher throughput, powered mincers can process larger pieces of raw material, and thus save valuable butchers' time.

Powered mincers are produced in varying sizes, from bench or table-mounted, single speed models with capacities of 85 kg per hour, to automatic, double-feeding, dual-speed models capable of handling pre-broken frozen meat up to 6,000 kg per hour (these mincers are often referred to as grinders). A manufacturer should choose a machine whose quoted output is higher than production requirements since these continuously rated outputs are often only realised under ideal conditions. A mincer suitable for small-scale pork processing operations is shown in figure III.2.

II.2 Mixers/blenders

Mixers and blenders, although often used for the same task, are distinctly different in the way they function. Mixers simply mix the product

Figure III.2

Mincer for small-scale pork processing

to incorporate all of the ingredients. Blenders, on the other hand, mix the product and perform the necessary mechanical agitation required for product binding.

Mixers are round-bottomed tanks equipped with wing-shaped paddles revolving in opposite directions. They vary in size from 12-litre bowl capacity, bench-mounted models (see figure III.3) to 7,000-litre models fitted with pneumatically operated discharge hatches and bucket lifting hoists. The small mixers with a bowl capacity of 12-30 litres are suitable for small-scale processing operations.

Some companies supply equipment where the mincing and mixing functions are incorporated into one single machine. This equipment facilitates production and eliminates the need for manual manipulation of the minced ingredients.

II.3 Cutters/bowl choppers

In a cutter or bowl chopper, comminution and mixing of the meat ingredients are accomplished by revolving the meat in a bowl past a series of knives mounted on a fixed shaft that rotates at high speed. The meat is guided to the knives via a plough shaped arrangement fitted on to the side of the bowl (see figure III.4). In sophisticated cutters, bowl rotation, knife speed and temperature may be controlled and vacuum hoods fitted to enable chopping under vacuum.

To ensure correct cutting, the knives must be carefully adjusted and set as instructed by the manufacturer. The action of the knives raises the temperature of the meat. If the latter is allowed to become too warm, the characteristics of the emulsion will be lost. Cutting time should be regulated through careful control of temperature.

Bowl choppers range in size and complexity from a 10-litre, single knife model to a 500-litre, multiple knives vacuum model. There are various combinations in all capacities. The purchase of this piece of equipment should be made with great care since the ease of product manufacture depends upon it. Single knife choppers are satisfactory for the single product manufacturer, especially where the cutting process can be interrupted to allow for additional cooling. For the production of a variety of chopped products, a multiple blade, two-speed instrument is essential.

Figure III.3

Mixer suitable for small-scale pork processing

- 35 -

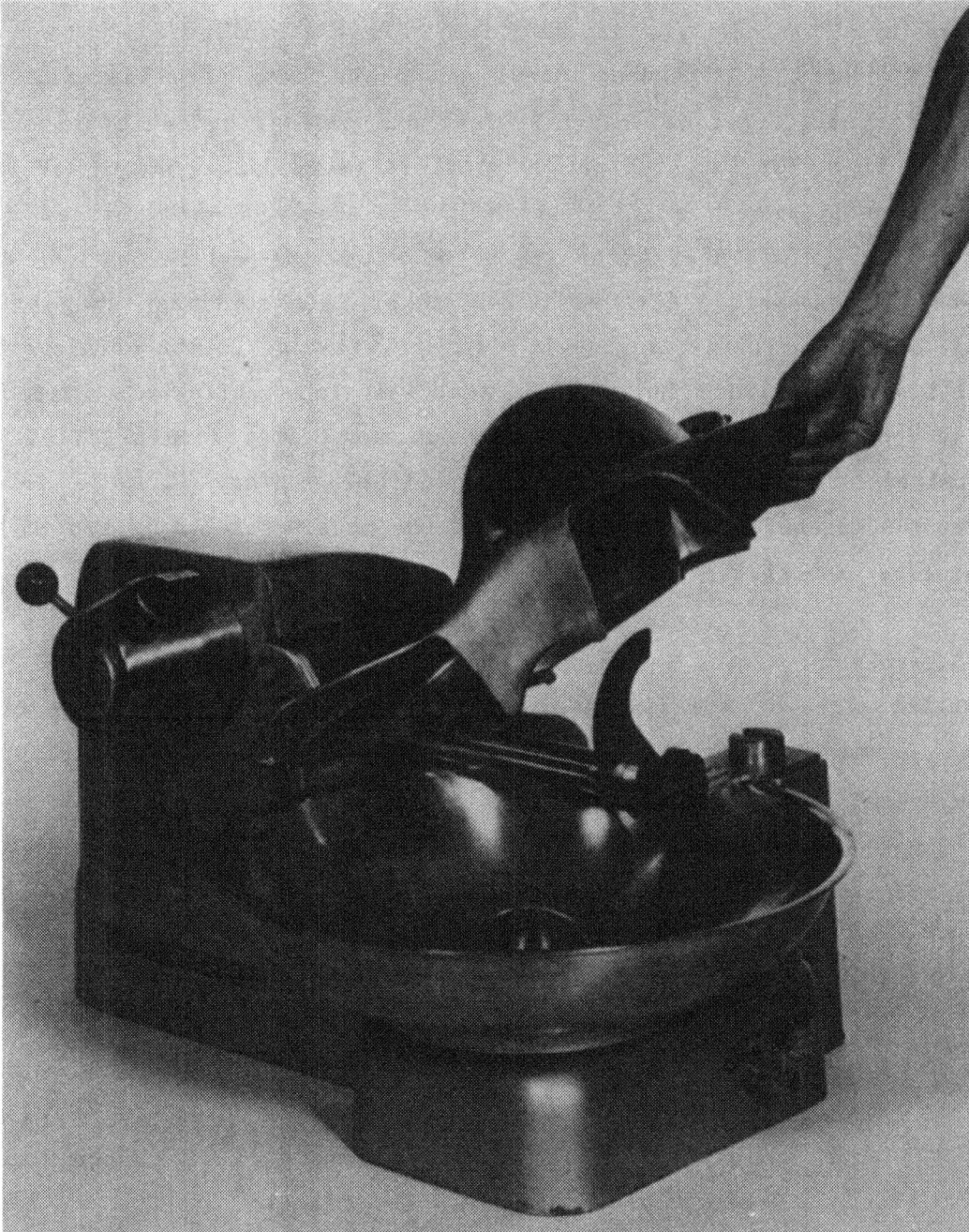

Figure III.4
10-litre capacity bowl cutter, with single blade

In all cases, the machine should be demonstrated under production conditions before a final selection is made.

II.4 Extruders/stuffers

There are two types of extruders: the pump type and the stuffer type. The pump type extruder is usually used for high-volume (1-5 tonnes/hour) fine-cut products. It cannot handle coarsely chopped emulsions. Piston stuffers fill all types of meat mixtures into casings or other containers if used carefully. The larger capacity stuffers (e.g. 250 kg/hour) are vertical cylinders equipped with a cover which can be removed or tightened quickly. These cylinders contain a piston which moves upwards and forces meat through an opening in the side, just below the cover into stuffing tubes or horns. Various linking and portioning devices may be attached to the opening to speed up filling. Various horizontal, small-scale stuffers equipped with manually-controlled pistons are also manufactured (see figure III.5). These are suitable for very small operations (50-75 kg/day) but do involve a considerable degree of manual handling of the meat. Careful regard to hygiene is therefore essential.

II.5 Ice-maker

Chilled water or ice flakes are added at the cutting stage in order to keep the comminuted meat from overheating. For small-scale operations, ice can be purchased from the nearest ice plant. It is incorporated into meat products in the flake or crushed form to maximise 'cold transfer'. Any surplus ice can be used for cold brine make-up, thus saving on cold store duty and space. All ice used in meat processing operations should be prepared from treated water.

Ice-making plants with capacities of 70 kg per 24 hours and higher are available. All of them incorporate stainless steel lined bins to hold the ice and most plants are fitted with automatic controls to start ice-making and shut off the unit when the bin is filled. The ice-maker requires a supply of treated water.

II.6 Brine injectors

Single-lance or multi-lance brine injectors are used by the meat processing industry to pump brines of any desired concentration into meat tissues. Extremely good brine distribution may be achieved by relatively

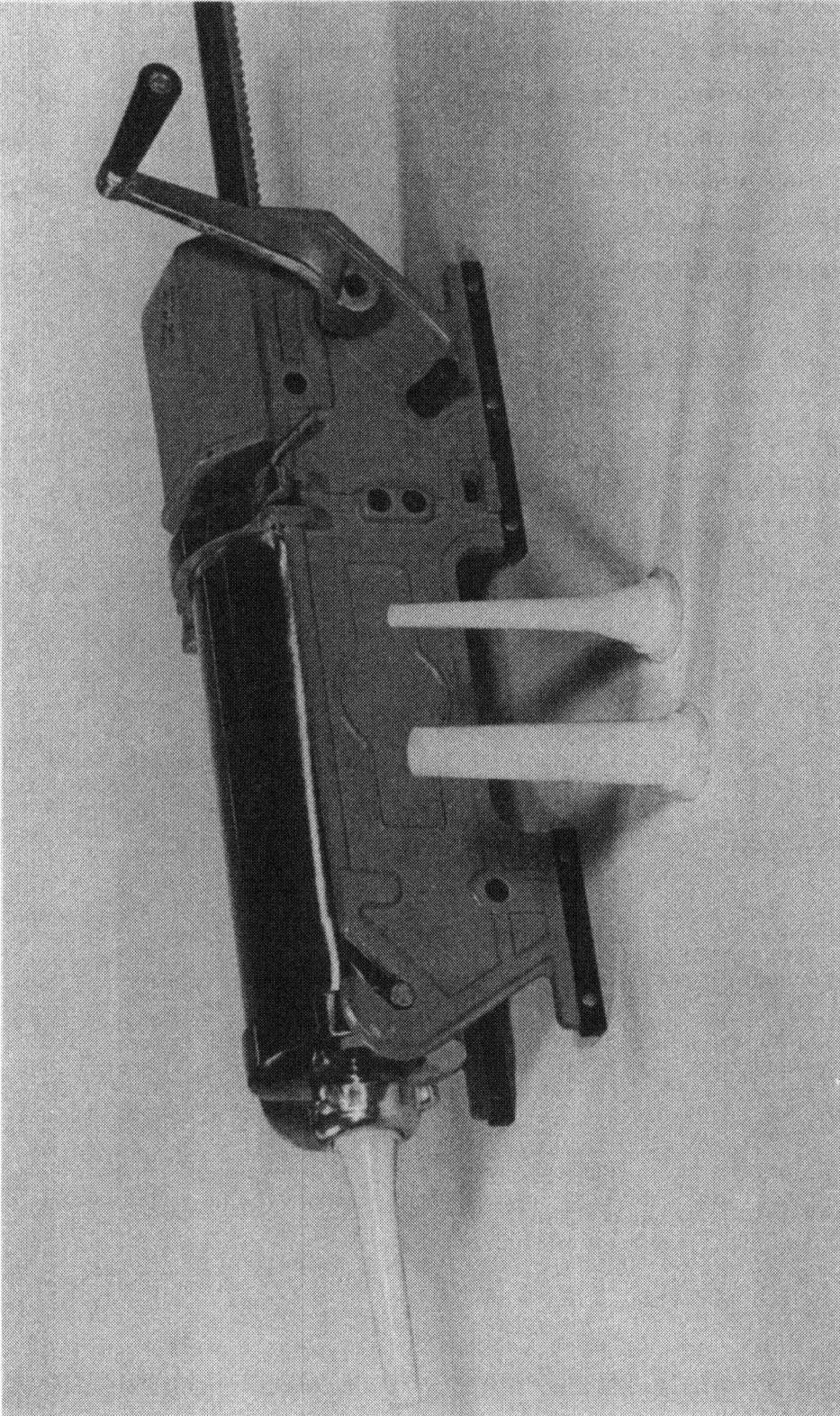

Figure III.5

Horizontal stuffer, manually operated

unskilled operators. The simplest type of injector, such as that shown in figure III.6, uses a single needle with a number of holes along its length. The machine is designed for hand operation. Automatic, multi-needle injectors offering the processor an opportunity for rapid processing are also available. Such models would not be suitable for small-scale operations. Brine injection systems can be used in combination with dry salt or wet-soaking curing procedures.

II.7 Meat tumblers/massagers

With the advent of comminuted ham products, which are essentially "solid sausages" made from whole pieces of meat, it is necessary to increase the binding capacity of the various meat components. This is done by tumbling - also called massaging - the meat chunks for a limited time in a solution which solubilises certain proteins. This operation induces binding between the pieces and increases the water uptake of the meat.

A tumbler is a stainless steel drum which revolves slowly, often under vacuum, through a programmed series of revolutions. Capacities range from the small-scale unit of 130 litres to the large-scale unit of 2,000 litres which handles bacon sides.

Tumbling increases water uptake of the meat and can, under certain circumstances, enable retention in the final product of 10-15 per cent extra (or added) water. By increasing the binding capacity, products can be made from lower quality meats. Both properties can obviously increase the profit margin of the processor. While tumbling is a relatively recent innovation in meat processing, it is of interest to developing countries where the binding capacity of often poor quality meat can be increased. This can thus be incorporated into high quality meat products.

II.8 Meat/bacon slicers

Slicers are used by meat processors to prepare sliced pork products for immediate sale. Gravity fed models are available to enable operators to slice all boneless meats without the need to feed the product manually on to the blade. The slicing blade is kept sharp by an adjustment sharpening stone that sits over the blade while it is in operation. Most models feature dial type, self-locking slice thickness regulators and spiked feed grips to clamp on irregular-shaped pieces of meat.

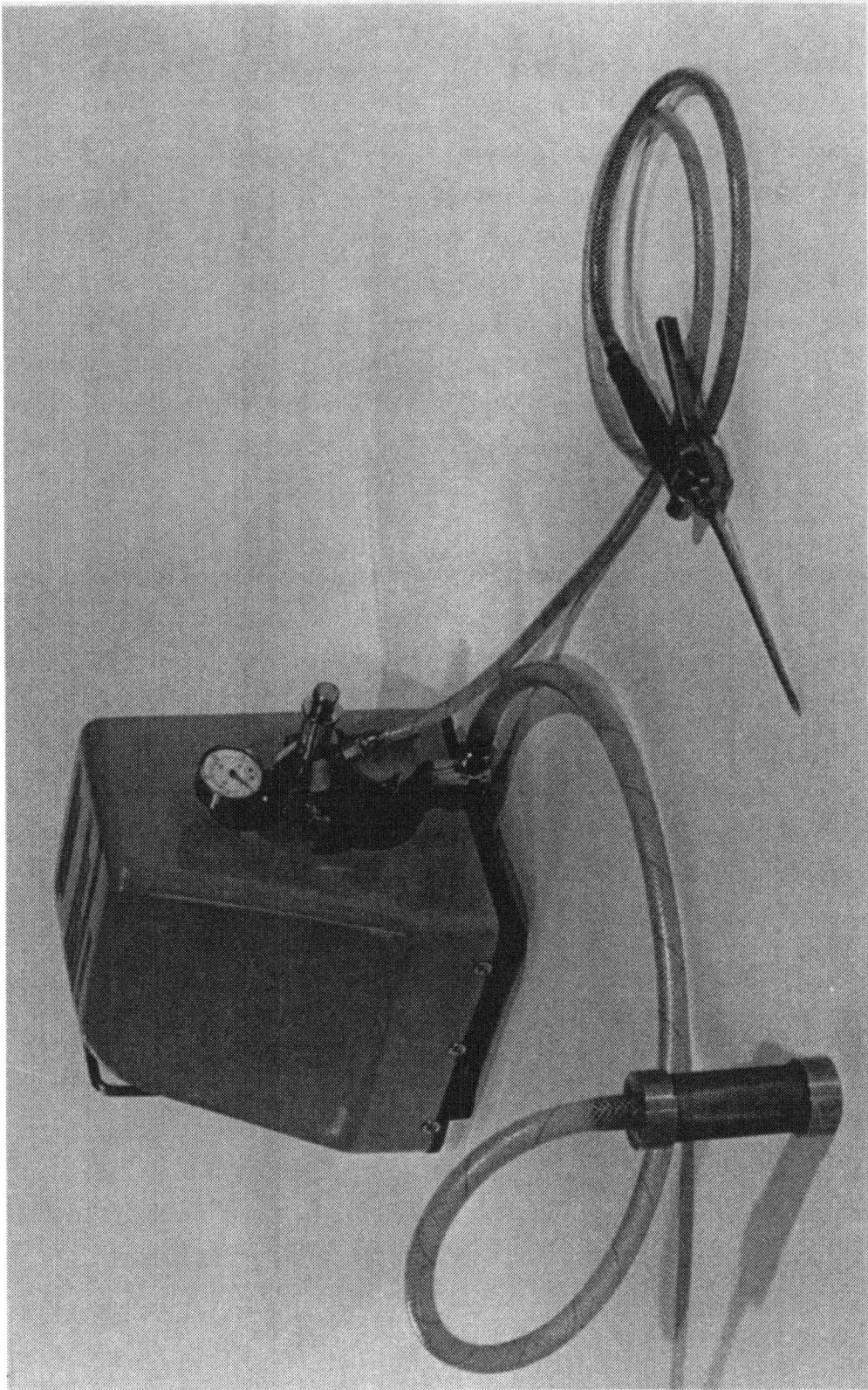

Figure III.6

Single-lance brine injector

II.9 Smokehouses/processing ovens

In addition to providing a chamber for the smoking of meat and meat products to an acceptable colour and flavour, modern smokehouses/processing ovens are also designed to perform the critical process of heating and cooking.

Control of temperature rise in products is very important. For example, all of the bacon lean tissue must receive sufficient heat to develop the red cured meat colour, yet the temperature must not be allowed to rise high enough to oversoften the fat. Failure may result from a deviation of 3-5°C from the theoretical processing temperature. The smokehouse temperature must be limited to a few degrees centigrade about the final internal meat temperature. Extended heating times of 12-24 hours are therefore required for bacon even though the smoking operation is carried out for only a part of the time (e.g. 2-8 hours).

Smoking and cooking operations are under continual review and a number of improved plant designs are now commercially available. Most modern plants employ smoke generators, comprising a box or drum equipped with a mechanical agitator and blower to draw smoke across the product. The simplest possible system consists of a pile of damp hardwood sawdust which is burnt under or alongside the smokehouse. Another type of smoke generator is also available. It uses dry sawdust which is fed into a small, electrically heated chamber and burned in air to an ash. This type of generator yields a high volume of smoke for the amount of sawdust used but requires more maintenance than the wet sawdust models.

Figure III.7 illustrates a simple type of smokehouse with a working volume of 1 m^3 (equivalent to 50 kg of sausage product) which could be built from local materials. Its performance as a cold smoking unit could be improved by the addition of an internal fan, thereby creating convection currents within the unit. Thermostatically controlled electric heating can be installed to enable the kiln to be used for hot smoking (i.e. partial cooking). Cooking can be completed in cooking kettles. Products are moved to and from the unit by mobile trolleys which may also be produced locally.

Specialist products, such as frankfurters, require a more sophisticated control of smoking and cooking procedures for consistent quality. In this case, the cooking and smoking operations are combined in the same equipment. This type of air-conditioned smokehouse is illustrated in figure III.8.

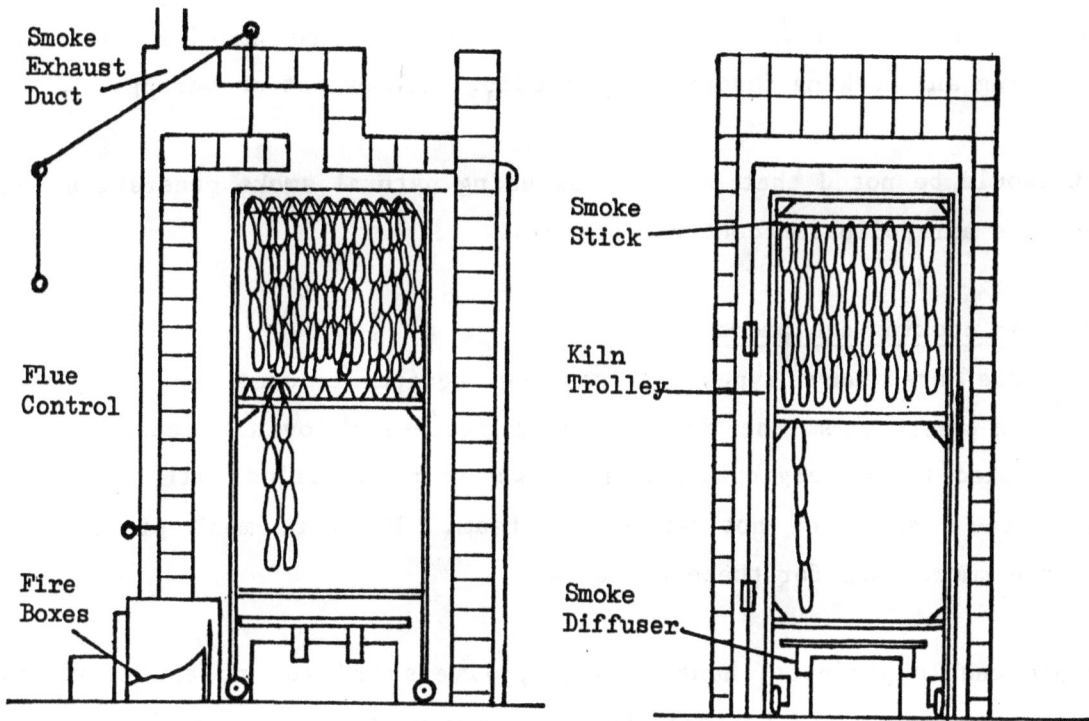

Figure III.7

Simple, masonry-type smokehouse

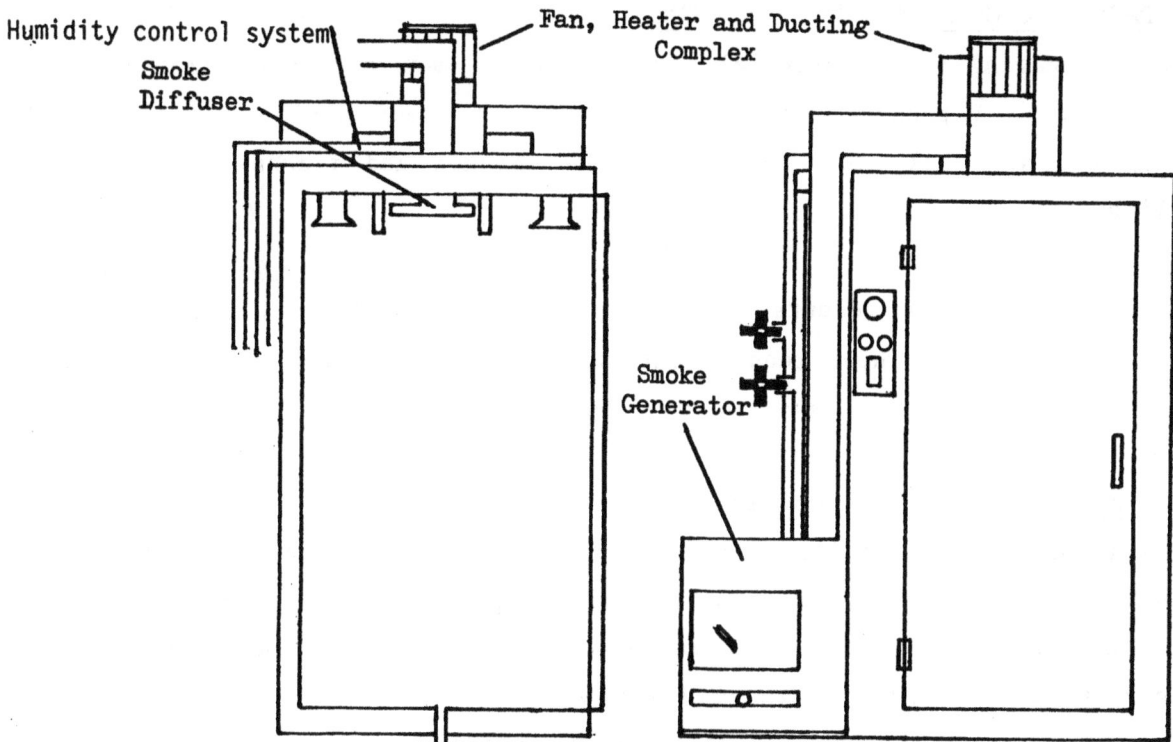

Figure III.8

Air-conditioned smokehouse and processing oven

The regulation of temperature, humidity and volume of circulated air and the density of smoke is accomplished by varying the amount of outside air or by injecting steam into the house. This type of smokehouse (or processing oven, as it is often called), can perform, in addition to smoking, all of the conditioning and cooking functions, including cold or hot showering.

It should be noted that smokehouses using natural smoke generators require appropriate air pollution control equipment.

II.10 Other cooking equipment

There are many types of cooking equipment used in pork product manufacture apart from the multi-purpose processing oven. Sausage products may be cooked by submerging them in tanks or pans filled with water, or by exposure to a spray of hot water or steam. However, most processors now employ the smokehouse for these products.

Whole muscle products, hams, tongues, livers and so on, are often cooked in steam-jacketed, round bottomed kettles made of stainless steel. Live steam or electrically heated kettles are now available. Ham cookers are available to suit particular moulds and product loads, so that cooking can be closely controlled to minimise losses. (See figure III.9).

III. PACKAGING MATERIALS AND EQUIPMENT

Good packaging is an essential element in the manufacture of high quality pork products. A package must not only protect goods during transport and handling but also help to preserve good appearance and freshness throughout retailing.

The packaging requirements of fresh, cured and processed pork products differ considerably. These requirements are briefly reviewed below for fresh products and cured and processed meats respectively.

III.1 Fresh meat and fresh pork sausages

Fresh pork sausages and ground pork rely on oxygen for the development of a bright red colour. They are usually sold wrapped in oxygen permeable films such as cellophane, polyvinyl chloride and polyethylene. Prolonged storage at refrigerated temperatures in these films will however result in irreversible colour and flavour changes as well as microbial spoilage. For long-term storage, wrapped fresh pork sausage should be packed into cardboard boxes and frozen at -18°C.

Figure III.9
Steam-jacketed, round bottomed kettle

III.2 Cured and processed meats

The pigments in cured and processed meats are stable only in the absence of oxygen. It is essential, therefore, that these items be packaged in low oxygen transmitting material. Sliced products are particularly affected by exposure to air and light. Packaging in low oxygen permeable films such as polyester, polyamide and vinylidene chloride is acceptable for short-term storage of cured and processed pork products where vacuum packaging machinery is not available. Shrink films and stretch films improve product appearance and are generally preferred to simple bagging or overwrapping methods. For long-term packaging of cured meat, vacuum packaging is recommended. Vacuum sealing of products in bags or pouches made of plastic laminates (e.g. nylon and polyethylene) may be carried out in vacuum chambers or by the more simple evacuation and clip sealing machine. The latter consists of a screened vacuum pump working through a clipping nozzle. The material to be packed is enclosed in a laminate outer, presented to the nozzle and the vacuum established. This is accomplished within five to 30 seconds, depending on the air content of the pouch. On completion of evacuation, the pouch is clip-sealed and may be passed through a 'shrink wrapping tunnel' for better presentation. Capacities of the unit range from five packs to 15 packs per minute.

Vacuum chamber models consist of an impulse heat sealer working within a vacuum chamber. The material to be packed is carefully placed in the laminate (heat-sealable) pouch and the open end placed on the heat sealer. Closure of the chamber grips the open end, and the chamber is evacuated to a preset residual air level. In large machines, the chamber and product can be gas flushed (usually by nitrogen gas) at this stage. This procedure extends the vacuum pack shelf life. When the pressure inside the pouch is equal to the pressure in the chamber, the head sealer operates and closes the pack.

The chamber size determines the pack capacity that can be used. There is thus a very wide range of chamber sizes. The smallest, multi-purpose model in a table top version has a chamber volume of 0.03 m^3, with an impulse seal length of 0.4 m. This machine is supplied complete with a vacuum pump, and is capable of packing two small hams (5 kg each) at approximately one per minute. Single chamber machines rise in 0.01 m^3 stages up to a 0.15 m^3 model which has two sealing bars of 880 mm and 450 mm. Double chamber models are available in sizes starting at 0.045 m^3 which can pack six large hams (12 kg each) per minute. Although chamber type sealing is becoming more common (in particular for frankfurters and sliced, ready-to-serve meats), the alternative evacuation and clip sealing machine is cheaper and perhaps more appropriate for small-scale operations.

All items should be packaged in cardboard cartons ready for dispatch. The use of standard pallets is recommended for the mechanised handling of large deliveries. Packaged products should be removed from the processing plant and delivered to retail outlets immediately. The product should be refrigerated as far as possible throughout the marketing chain and should not be exposed to bright light for long periods.

One last cautionary note must be made regarding packaging. Good packaging is an expensive operation which may be omitted if the product is for immediate delivery to clients after processing and if no active competition exists in the processed meat market. On the other hand, if marketing delays cannot be avoided or if the product must compete against imports or other locally produced goods, good packaging may become a requirement. In this latter case, it may be worthwhile to use attractive and efficient packaging if this may result in larger sales. In all cases, the extra expense on attractive packaging must be weighed carefully against benefits derived from additional sales.

IV. LABELLING

The need for labelling is a function of the characteristics of the potential market and of the local legislation. Labelling may not be avoided if the products are to be marketed among middle- or high-income groups or are to be exported. In this case, labels play two important roles: they satisfy the need for information by literate consumers and custom officials and act as an incentive to purchase a particular product or brand. Some developing countries also require that all processed meat products be labelled. On the other hand, labelling may not be needed if goods are retailed without packaging, if the majority of the potential consumers are not literate, or if no competition exists.

In case labelling is required, the following general principles should be applied:

- The label should be legible and indelible. Hand written labels can be used where only a small amount of information needs to be communicated to the customer. Printed labels are advantageous in that they are clearer and allow the provision of more information. With printed labels, the layout can be planned in such a way as to emphasise important aspects of the product. Often, the consumer selects a product on the basis of name, weight, etc. If the selling point of the product is, for instance, its value per unit weight, weight information and price could be given prominence to attract the customer's attention.

- The label should be informative. In developed countries, legislation usually dictates the minimum amount of information to be carried on the label. Developing countries are becoming more aware of labelling requirements, particularly with respect to imported food goods. Thus, most countries have enacted legislation or guide-lines which dictate what should be carried on the label. Reference to the Ministry of Agriculture of the country concerned will usually clarify the situation regarding the minimum labelling requirements. In general, these include the following categories:

- product description (e.g. Fresh Pork Sausage). The name under which a product is sold should also include particulars as to the physical condition of the product or any specific treatment undergone by the product (e.g. freeze-dried, smoked);

- weight: Gross weight or net weight (gross weight minus wrapping or carton weight), or weight when packed if losses are likely in subsequent handling (e.g. bacon in cheesecloth wrapping);

- ingredients: These are usually in descending order of weight, as recorded at the time of their use in the manufacture of the foodstuff;

- origin: the name or business name, and address of the manufacturer, packer or seller, and the country of origin. One may also include in this category the packing station code (if any) and date of packing; and

- durability: Data on subsequent handling by the consumer (e.g. whether the product is stable at ambient temperatures or must be refrigerated) and conditions of use if these vary with time (e.g. minimum shelf life).

-The label must be accurate. The label must not deliberately mislead the consumer. Ingredients listing in meat products is attracting great attention largely because of the difficulty of detecting adulterant meats in the product after processing. In addition, the tendency of processors to add water has led to its inclusion on the ingredients list in the European Economic Community. This presents processors with a problem since most of the water is absorbed in an uncontrolled manner, particularly in fast-curing processes. It should be noted that an ingredient which is used in a foodstuff in a dried, dehydrated or concentrated state may be placed in the ingredients list as though it had first been reconstituted. If this is the case, the ingredient should be followed by the description "when reconstituted".

-Excessive labelling and detail should be avoided. The Government should ensure that the prevailing legislation on labelling protects both customers and retailers and allows for fair comparison between products.

V. PROCESSING PLANT HYGIENE

A regular cleaning routine for plant, equipment and premises is essential if a high level of plant hygiene is to be guaranteed.

Wood is often a preferred surface for cutting, deboning and chopping meat. However, wooden tables or chopping blocks are very difficult to cleanse thoroughly and are not recommended. A metal table with a high density polypropylene cutting inset affords equal protection to the edges of knives and tools and is far easier to clean.

Filling nozzles, knives, plates and so on, and the surfaces of mincers, mixers and bowl choppers require particular attention. Cleansing should involve a rough scrubbing with a brush fitted with nylon bristles to remove scraps of fat and should be followed by a thorough cleaning with a suitable bactericidal agent. Water for scrubbing down should be hot (around 82°C) and cleaning cloths should be boiled at the end of each day.

A 0.4 per cent sodium hypochlorite solution is effective for washing equipment, floors and walls. This solution should be thoroughly washed away with fresh water within ten minutes, to avoid corrosion of the equipment. The solution may be made up by adding 50 g of chloride of lime and 100 g of washing soda to a little cold water. The resultant paste is made up to 5 litres with water and, after settling, the clear 0.4 per cent hypochlorite solution is decanted off. The solution must be used on the day of manufacture if its powerful bactericidal properties are not to be lost. Care must be taken to ensure that the chloride of lime is not left to absorb moisture from the air. It should be kept in an airtight container.

Although cleaning schedules for plant and equipment can be arranged, it is often much more difficult to ensure that the staff comply with hygiene regulations. To reduce the risk of contamination, hot water and soap or disinfectant should be not only available but readily accessible. Education in hygiene among the work force is essential. No outdoor clothing or footwear should be allowed in the processing area and boiler suits and aprons should be changed daily, or more frequently if they become extremely soiled. All personnel, including managers should wear some type of head cover and should wash hands and arms thoroughly before entering the meat processing area. Smoking and eating should be prohibited in this area and all staff should be prevented from wearing jewellery or other adornment. Workers complaining of diarrhoea or stomach pains or showing signs of skin infection or boil, should be sent home for treatment immediately.

The manager is also responsible for taking all reasonable steps in order to keep the premises clear of rats, mice, birds and insects. Direct control of flying insects during processing may be limited to using ultra-violet light traps or fly screens. The treatment of effluents is also effective in preventing the massing of flies in the roof area. The spraying of the processing plant with a suitable insecticide (e.g. Pybuthrin) each evening will go some way towards dealing with insect populations.

CHAPTER IV

PROCESSING TECHNOLOGY

Buildings and equipment for small-scale pig-meat processing plants were described in the previous chapter for the manufacture of representative commodities from the major classes of products. Full processing details for this range of products are provided in this chapter.

The scope of the production activities is determined by a number of factors. Limited market opportunities and traditional local demand may restrict the manufacturer to the production of only one or two specific products. On the other hand, a retailer or hotelier used to imported brands may insist on the supply of a complete range of processed products. A small-scale producer should, as far as possible, be able to vary the nature of his operations accordingly.

The selection of product range should also reflect the nature of the raw materials which are available. High quality items, such as hams and some continental style sausages, cannot be manufactured from trimmings produced by the dressing of fresh pork. Conversely, the use of hindquarter and loin cuts for the manufacture of lower-quality fresh sausages would be financially unjustifiable.

The following information is provided for each meat product:

- the type of meat cuts and trimmings used in the product;
- the exact recipe for a given batch of finished product, including all spices, ice, casings and so on;
- the fractions of each ingredient per unit of output, and the yield on carcase meat "bone-in";

- a description of all processing steps, including overall processing times, and detailed processing times whenever necessary; and
- a flow diagram summarising the various steps in product preparation.

I. FRESH SAUSAGE

Fresh sausages are made from selected cuts of fresh meat that have not been previously cured. They must be kept under refrigeration and thoroughly cooked before being eaten.

I.1 Ingredients

Two sources of raw materials may be used for fresh sausage manufacture: pork derived from boning whole carcases (either hot or cold), usually from the flank and the neck, and selected trimmings from pork cutting operations. The ratio of lean to fat meat has an important bearing on the taste and texture of the sausage. In some countries, a white coloured fat pork sausage is preferred to a lean, red one. In general, fat levels should be held between 24 and 40 per cent to ensure good palatability. It must be remembered that lean trimmings may contain up to 30 per cent fat and that fat levels in regular trimmings may reach 60 per cent.

Figure IV.1 shows the parts of the carcase used for the preparation of first- and second-choice fresh sausages.

The freshness of the raw materials is the key to an acceptable product. Old, bruised or dirty trimmings should not be used. Frozen trimmings are permissible providing they were of good quality and well handled prior to freezing. All meat should be chilled between $2°C$ and $3°C$ except in the case of hot-boned material. Gristle, bone and cartilage should be carefully removed from trimmings taken from the blade, breast and neck regions. Table IV.1 provides the quantities of the various ingredients for the preparation of a given batch (20.6 kg) of two types of fresh sausages as well as the percentage of each ingredient per unit weight of finished product.

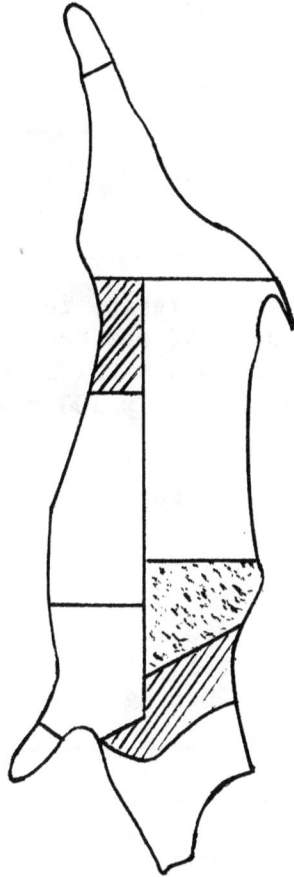

//// First choice

Second choice

Figure IV.1

Fresh sausage materials

Table IV.1

Ingredients for the production of fresh sausage

Ingredients	Quantity of ingredients per 20.6 kg batch	Percentage of each ingredient
A. Fresh sausage (Type 1)		
Lean pork	15 kg	72.82
Back fat	5 kg	24.27
Salt	415 g	2.01
Ground white pepper	75 g	0.36
Ground nutmeg	10 g	0.05
Ground sage	25 g	0.13
Dextrose	75 g	0.36
Casings (narrow pig)	70 m	
Total ingredients (less casings)	20.6 kg	100.00

Yield on finished product[1]: 100 per cent on recipe ingredients
Estimated carcase cut-out of meat inputs[2]: 90 per cent
Carcase meat "bone-in" required[3] : 20 kg ÷ 0.9 = 22.22 kg
Yield on carcase meat "bone-in"[4]:(20.6 ÷ 22.22) x 100 = 93 per cent

B. Fresh sausage (Type 2)		
Lean pork	13 kg	63.00
Back fat	4.5 kg	21.81
Cereals	1.3 kg	6.30
Ice	1.3 kg	6.30
Salt and spices as for type 1	350 g	1.70
Sugar	185 g	0.89
Total ingredients	20.6 kg	100.00

Yield on finished product : 100 per cent on recipe ingredients
Estimated carcase cut-out of meat inputs: 90 per cent
Carcase meat "bone-in" required: 17.5 kg ÷ 0.9 = 19.44 kg
Yield on carcase meat "bone-in" : (20.6 ÷ 19.44) x 100 = 106 per cent.

I.2 Processing stages

Mincing

Mincing prepares the material for easy mixing with the spices. Trimmings and pork cuts are normally passed through a coarse 12 mm plate mincer before the fat is added. The meat and fat are then passed though a 4 mm plate mincer. It is a normal procedure to cool the materials between mincing

[1] This is equal to the weight of output divided by the total weight of inputs, multiplied by 100.
[2] This is an estimate based on butchery practice.
[3] This is equal to the weight of the meat inputs (lean beef, trimmings and fat) divided by the estimated carcase cut-out of meat inputs.
[4] This is equal to the weight of the output divided by the weight of carcase

stages. Furthermore, the knives on the mincer should be kept sharp to minimise the crushing of the meat and keep the temperature as low as possible.

Mixing

The ground pork is placed in a mixer together with salt, pepper and sage (or any other spices, according to local tastes) and thoroughly mixed. Dextrose is added to enhance flavour and improve the red colour of the lean meat. Excessive mixing after the salt has been added can cause too much extraction of the soluble proteins and result in a rubbery end product.

Stuffing

After the meat has been mixed with the spices, it is placed in a stuffer and extruded into narrow or medium sheep or pork casings. The casings should be soaked in fresh water for one to two hours, and then cut into appropriate lengths (depending on stuffer capacity), before being placed on the stuffing horn. A plump product, free of air pockets, should be aimed for. A table or bench should be placed under the outlet of the stuffing horn to support the casing as it is filled and to facilitate subsequent linking. One kg of fresh sausage mix will fill approximately 3 m of medium sheep casings or 3.5 m of narrow pork casings.

Linking

When all the material has passed into the casing, the end of the latter should be tied off, and the tube divided into links by twisting at regular intervals. The length of the link depends on market demand. Continuous stuffers are usually equipped with a linking device as well as a partitioner to provide links of exact weight.

Packaging and handling

Unless the sausages are for immediate sale, the product should be stored at -18°C. Fresh sausages are usually cellophane wrapped in units of 500 g, 1 kg, 2 kg or 5 kg, with a date of production clearly shown. They may also be wholesaled unwrapped if transported in hygienic seamless metal or plastic lidded containers.

For type 2 sausage, all stages are similar except mixing: the minced pork is placed in the mixer, and cereal and ice added and mixed briefly. Spices and salt are then added and mixing continued until a homogeneous firm product is obtained. The complete production sequence is illustrated in figure IV.2.

ESTIMATE MEAT REQUIREMENT   ESTIMATE CASING REQUIREMENT

PRIMAL BUTCHERY   CASINGS
                                        (Narrow pig)
Flank, neck

DEBONE   SOAK 25°C, 2 hrs

Regular trimmings   Meat   Fat

Weigh out to give 75% lean,
25% fat

Regular trimmings   Meat   Fat

MINCE 12 mm

(CHILL)

Weigh out spices, salt, dextrose

MINCE 4 mm

Salt
Spices   MIX   DRAIN
Dextrose

Prepare stuffer

STUFF (3 m per kg)

LINK (according to trade

PACK (cellophane or sealed bin)

DISPATCH   STORE 0°C will last 1 day
                        -18°C if not for immediate sale

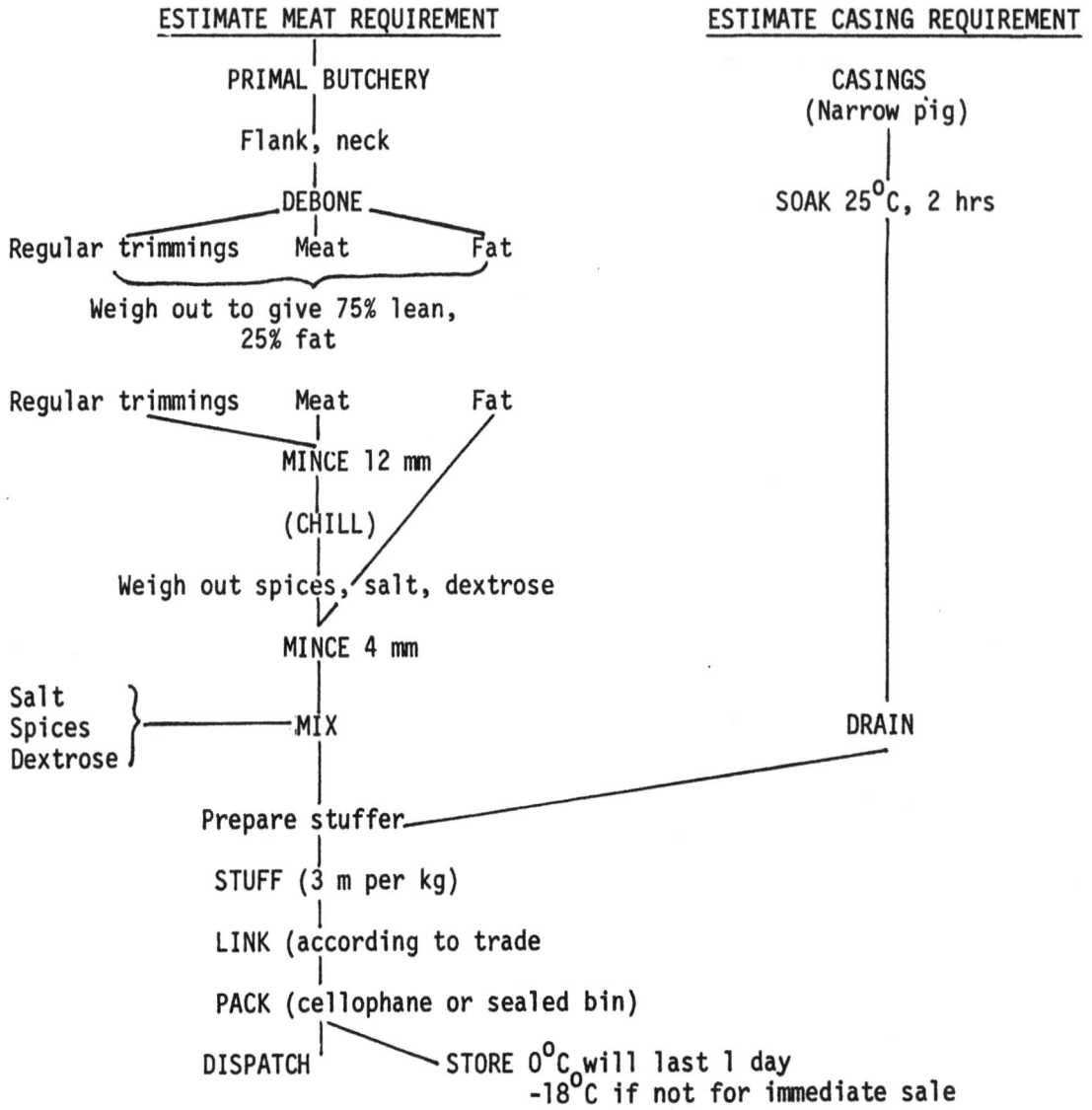

Processing time: 4 hrs

Figure IV.2
Flow diagram illustrating fresh sausage preparation

II UNCOOKED SMOKED SAUSAGE

Uncooked, smoked sausage differs from fresh pork sausage only in that the meat is subjected to a mild cure and smoked. Included in this group are tea sausage, Metwurst, smoked Thuringer, Polish sausage (Kielbasa) and Italian pork sausage. All products must be cooked before serving although in some cases this is carried out by the processor.

II.1 Ingredients

Smoked pork sausage is made from lean pork, usually containing 75 per cent lean meat. Trimmed meat from the shoulder, hand and leg cuts is most suitable. Belly and flank meat should not be used because the high level of fat will cause the product to soften during smoking. See figure IV.3 for first- and second-choice meat cuts used in uncooked smoked sausage.

As with fresh sausage, great care must be taken to ensure the freshness of the raw materials. All cuts should be chilled between 2°C and 3°C, except in the case of hot-boned material. Pale, soft and exudative (PSE) pork should not be used.

Table IV.2 provides the quantities of ingredients used for the production of the following uncooked, smoked sausages:

  -tea sausage;
  -Metwurst;
  -Polish sausage;
  -Thuringer; and
  -Italian pork sausage.

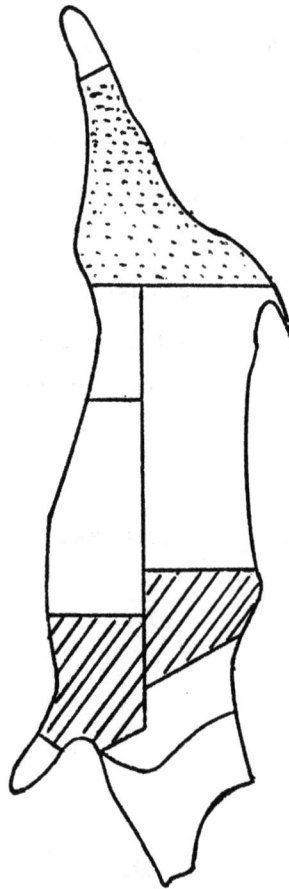

//// First choice

Second choice

Figure IV.3

Uncooked, smoked sausage material

Table IV.2

Ingredients for the production of various types of uncooked, smoked sausages

Ingredients	Quantity of ingredients per batch	Percentage of each ingredient
A. Tea sausage		
Lean pork	13.50 kg	65.08
Back fat	6.50 kg	31.33
Nitrite salt	600 g	2.89
Dextrose	60 g	
Ground black pepper	60 g	
Paprika	10 g	0.70
Ground coriander	05 g	
Ground mace	10 g	
Large hog casings	30 m	
Total ingredients (less casings)	20.745 kg	100.00

Yield on finished product: 96 per cent on recipe ingredients
Estimated carcase cut-out of meat inputs: 90 per cent
Carcase meat "bone-in" required = 20 kg ÷ 0.9 = 22.22 kg
Yield on carcase meat "bone-in" (20.745 ÷ 22.22) x 0.96 = 90 per cent

Ingredients	Quantity of ingredients per batch	Percentage of each ingredient
B. Metwurst		
Lean pork	11.00 kg	53.21
Regular pork trimmings	5.00 kg	24.19
Lean trimmings	4.00 kg	19.35
Salt	5.00 kg	2.42
Ground white pepper	75 g	
Ground caraway seed	12 g	
Mustard	38 g	0.83
Ground cloves	6 g	
Ground coriander	25 g	
Sage	6 g	
Large hog casings	30 m	
Total ingredients (less casings)	20.671 kg	100.00

Yield of finished product: 95 per cent of recipe ingredients
Estimated carcase cut-out of meat inputs: 90 per cent
Carcase meat "bone-in" required: 20 ÷ 0.9 = 22.22 kg
Yield on carcase meat "bone-in" : (20.671 ÷ 22.22) x 0.95 = 88 per cent

Ingredients	Quantity of ingredients per batch	Percentage of each ingredient
C. Polish sausage		
Lean pork	15.00 kg	72.34
Pork back-fat	5.00 kg	24.11
Nitrite salt	600 g	2.89
Ground black pepper	100 g	
Ground coriander	20 g	0.66
Garlic powder	15 g	
Medium hog casings	40 m	
Total ingredients (less casings)	20.735 kg	100.00

Yield on finished product: 94 pe cent of recipe ingredients
Estimated carcase cut-out of meat inputs: 90 per cent
Carcase meat "bone-in" required: 20 ÷ 0.9 = 22.22 kg
Yield on carcase meat "bone-in" (20.735 ÷ 22.22) x 0.94 = 88 per cent

Table IV.2 (cont'd)

D. Thuringer

Lean pork	12.00 kg	58.16
Pork cheeks	3.00 kg	14.54
Regular pork trimmings	5.00 kg	24.23
Salt	420g	2.03
Sugar	87.5 g	
Ground mace	12.5 g	
Ground caraway	10 g	1.04
Ground ginger	13 g	
Ground black pepper	75 g	
Ground coriander	13 g	
Medium hog casings	40 m	
Total ingredients (less casings)	20.631 kg	100.00

Yield on finished product = 95 per cent of recipe ingredients
Estimated carcase cut-out of meat inputs= 90 per cent
Carcase meat "bone-in" required = 20 ÷ 0.9 = 22.22 kg
Yield on carcase meat "bone-in" = 20.631 ÷ 22.22) x 0.95 = 28 per cent

E. Italian pork sausage

Lean pork trimmings	20 kg	97.79
Salt	300 g	1.47
Ground white pepper	50 g	
Ground coriander	13 g	
Fennel	50 g	0.74
Ground paprika	25 g	
Ground red pepper(mild)	13 g	
Medium hog casings	40 m	
Total ingredients (less casings)	20.451 kg	100.00

Yield on finished product = 95 per cent of recipe ingredients
Estimated carcase cut-out of meat inputs = 90 per cent
Carcase meat "bone-in" required = 20 ÷ 0.9 = 22.22 kg
Yield on carcase meat "bone-in" = (20.451 ÷ 22.22) x 0.95 = 87 per cent

II.2 Processing stages

Until recently, most smoked sausages were sold uncooked. However, recent demand for a product of longer shelf life have led to the cooking of some types of sausages. In tropical locations, they should be sold cooked if uncertified meat is included. Cooking procedures are similar to those for frankfurters (see section IV).

Mincing and cutting

Uncooked, smoked sausages come in many varieties depending on the degree of initial comminution. Tea sausage and Metwurst are considered fine-cut sausages while Polish sausage and smoked Thuringer are coarse-cut varieties.

(i) Fine cut (e.g. tea sausage): The pork fat is first passed through a mincer fitted with a 2 mm-plate. It is then placed in a bowl chopper and cut for several revolutions (3 slow, 5 fast). The fat is removed and stored overnight in a chill room (2°C) in covered trays. (For the production of Metwurst, regular and lean pork trimmings are combined and minced through an 8 mm plate. One-quarter of the total salt is added and the mixture lightly mixed and reminced through a 2 mm plate. It is then held overnight in the chill room). The lean pork should be passed through a mincer fitted with an 8 mm plate and, after addition of the nitrite salt (or residual salt for Metwurst) and sugar, passed through a 2 mm plate. The minced pork should be held overnight at a temperature between 5°C and 8°C. The following day, the fat and minced pork (or trimmings and minced pork for Metwurst) should be mixed together in the bowl chopper and cut at high speed for 40 revolutions. Spices should be added during this final cutting.

(ii) Coarse cut (e.g. Polish sausage): The lean pork and back fat or meat/trimming combinations should be cut into small pieces (2 cm cubes) and chilled before passing through a mincer fitted with an 8 mm plate. Spices may be added either before or after mincing. The mixing process is critical and must be sufficient to extract the contractile proteins and provide the necessary bind. The meat is normally reminced through an 8 mm plate after mixing.

Stuffing

The size and nature of the casing used for these products depend upon he type of uncooked, smoked sausage being prepared. In the case of Metwurst and tea sausage, beef rounds (36-38 mm stuffed diameter) are used, while Thuringer and Polish sausage are normally prepared with medium or large hog casings (32-44 mm stuffed diameter).

When fine cut sausages are being stuffed, care is necessary to prevent the inclusion of air into the casing since air gives rise to grey spots. Casings are sometimes pricked to permit the air to escape.

Salted hog and beef casings should be soaked with water prior to being placed on the stuffing horn. This water is expelled from the casing by stripping between the fingers before it is stuffed. As the casing fills with meat it work itself off the stuffing horn on to a table placed immediately

Linking

When all the material has passed into the casing, the end should be tied off with good quality twine and the tube divided into links by twisting or tying off at regular intervals. The length of the link varies with market demand, but tea sausage and Polish sausage are usually marketed in 125 g portions.

Good quality medium hog casings are normally sold in links of 100 metres, with a minimum of 15 strands per link. One kilogram of sausage mix fills approximately 1.8 metres of medium hog casings.

Beef rounds are generally sold in sets containing a minimum of 30 metres. One kilogram of sausage mix fills approximately 1.5 metre of beef rounds, making up approximately eight sausages.

Maturation

Tea sausage and Metwurst are usually matured for between two and four days prior to smoking. In the case of tea sausage, the links are held in a chamber at 20-22°C and a relative humidity of 90 per cent for up to four days, while Metwurst is held at 16°C and a relative humidity of 75-80 per cent for two days. Some drying takes place during these maturation periods.

Smoking

After linking and maturing (where appropriate), the sausages are moved directly to the smokehouse. Smoking procedures vary according to the product and the type of plant available. Where possible, these pork products should be smoked at low temperatures (between 18°C and 21°C) over a period of approximately eight to 24 hours. The finished product should have an attractive golden yellow to chestnut colour and should have acquired a full flavour. After smoking, the products are allowed to dry for a further 24 hours in a room maintained at a temperature of between 16°C and 18°C.

Cooking

Smoked Thuringer sausage and Polish sausage are usually cooked before leaving the processing plant. Metwurst and tea sausage are not. The former should be cooked in a smokehouse at a temperature of between 65°C and 68°C until the internal temperature has reached 62°C. Care must be taken to ensure adequate air movement during cooking (by not overloading the smokehouse).

Packaging and storage

After cooking, the sausages are removed from the smokehouse and cooled at air or room temperature. The shelf-life of these products is improved if they are held under refrigeration throughout storage and marketing.

The complete production sequence for these meat products is illustrated in figure IV.4.

III. MORTADELLA

Mortadella is representative of a class of cooked sausages, all prepared according to similar processing procedures and known in Europe under the name of Bruhwurst. These sausages are made from a mixture of finely minced meat, fatty tissues and added water, nitrite curing salts, spices and spice extracts. Products are stuffed into casings after curing and may be sold smoked or unsmoked.

There are many types of mortadella sausage manufactured around the world. They vary not only in the appearance of the finished products but also in the nature of the raw materials used. Many types incorporate beef but the high quality sausage described here is made from pork meat alone.

III.1 Ingredients

Finished mortadella sausage should be light red in colour. Pork from fully matured hogs is preferred. Lean pork is taken from the shoulder and ham, with fat removed to 85 per cent lean. Both back fat and jowls should be diced in 50 mm cubes, mixed with 20 g of salt per kilo of material and kept in a cooler at $0°C$, overnight. The shoulder and belly of pork should also be held at $0°C$. On the day of manufacture, the back fat and jowl meat should be immersed in boiling water for 5 seconds and allowed to drain.

Figure IV.5 shows first- and second-choice meat cuts used for the production of mortadella, while table IV.3 provides the quantities of ingredients needed for a given batch (20.7 kg) of finished products.

III.2 Processing stages

Mincing
The jowl, belly and shoulder meat is minced through a 5-mm plate before

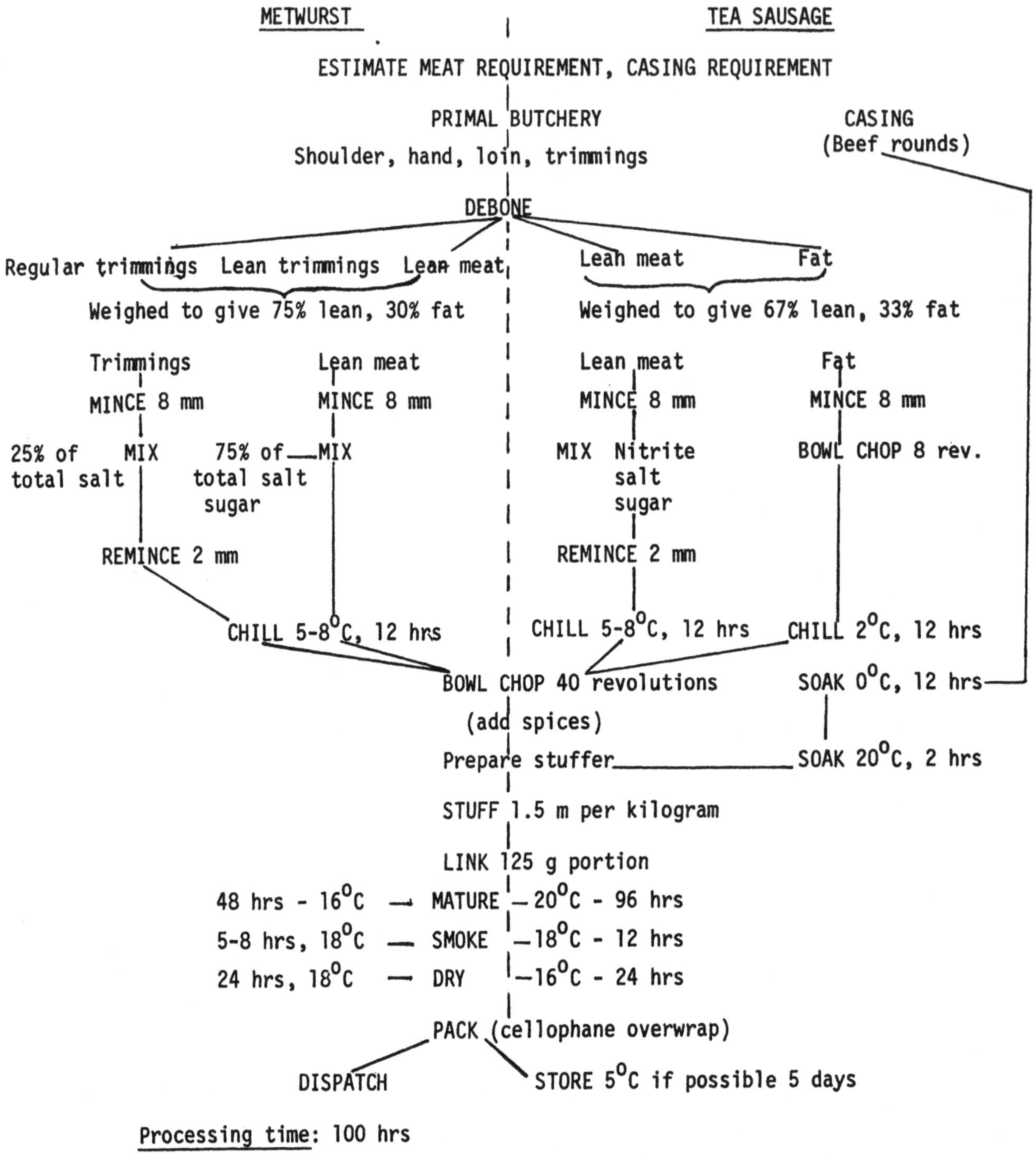

METWURST | TEA SAUSAGE

ESTIMATE MEAT REQUIREMENT, CASING REQUIREMENT

PRIMAL BUTCHERY

Shoulder, hand, loin, trimmings

CASING
(Beef rounds)

DEBONE

Regular trimmings Lean trimmings Lean meat | Lean meat Fat

Weighed to give 75% lean, 30% fat | Weighed to give 67% lean, 33% fat

Trimmings | Lean meat | Lean meat | Fat

MINCE 8 mm | MINCE 8 mm | MINCE 8 mm | MINCE 8 mm

25% of total salt MIX 75% of total salt sugar ─MIX | MIX Nitrite salt sugar | BOWL CHOP 8 rev.

REMINCE 2 mm | REMINCE 2 mm

CHILL 5-8°C, 12 hrs | CHILL 5-8°C, 12 hrs CHILL 2°C, 12 hrs

BOWL CHOP 40 revolutions | SOAK 0°C, 12 hrs

(add spices)

Prepare stuffer _____ SOAK 20°C, 2 hrs

STUFF 1.5 m per kilogram

LINK 125 g portion

48 hrs - 16°C ⟶ MATURE ─20°C - 96 hrs

5-8 hrs, 18°C ── SMOKE ─18°C - 12 hrs

24 hrs, 18°C ── DRY ─16°C - 24 hrs

PACK (cellophane overwrap)

DISPATCH ↘ STORE 5°C if possible 5 days

Processing time: 100 hrs

Figure IV.4

Flow diagram illustrating the preparation of uncooked,
smoked sausage

- 63 -

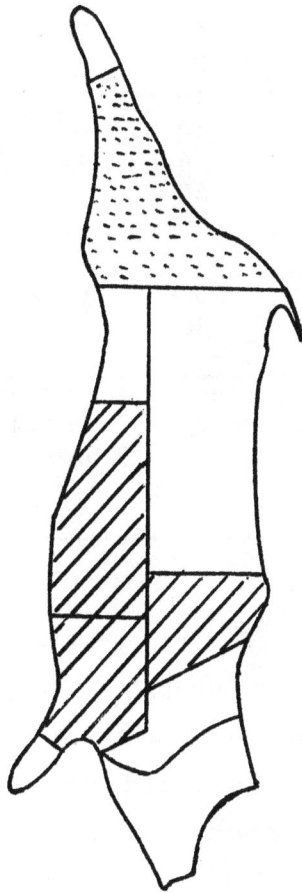

⧫⧫⧫⧫ First choice

⠂⠄⠂ Second choice

Figure IV.5

Mortadella materials

Table IV.3

Ingredients for the production of mortadella

Ingredients	Quantity of ingredients per 20.7 kg batch	Percentage of each ingredient
Lean pork	8.0 kg	38.65
Belly of pork	6.0 kg	28.98
Pork jowl	2.0 kg	9.66
Back fat	2.0 kg	9.66
Flake ice	2.0 kg	9.66
Ground white pepper	40 g	
Sweet paprika	30 g	
Ground mace	10 g	
Ground coriander	10 g	3.39
Ground ginger	6 g	
Cardamon	40 g	
Nitrite salt	500 g	
- Dextrose	10 g	
- Large hog casings	50 m	
Total ingredients (less casings)	20.7 kg	100.00

Yield on finished product : 80 per cent of recipe ingredient
Estimated carcase cut-out value of meat inputs = 92 per cent
Carcase meat "bone-in" required : 18 kg ÷ 0.92 = 19.56 kg
Yield on carcase meat "bone-in" : (20.7 ÷ 19.56) x 0.8 = 85 per cent

Cutting

The minced pork and flake ice are chopped for two minutes at low temperature. The remaining nitrite salt and sugar are then added and the whole mixture is chopped further at high speed until a fine emulsion is formed. Careful control of the temperature is essential during this phase and under no circumstances should it exceed 7-9°C. This can be monitored with a thermocouple fitted with a stainless steel sheathed probe. The spices and back fat are then added and chopping continued for several revolutions to ensure adequate mixing. The fat should not be cut too small (0.4-0.6 cm). Temperature rather than time is a better guide in chopping.

Maturation and stuffing

The emulsion is removed from the cutter and packed tightly into deep trays which must be covered and placed in a 2°C store overnight.

Mortadella sausages are usually filled into casings with a 10-20 cm stuffed diameter of 10-20 cm. Beef bungs (caecum) or beef bladders are normally used but hog bladders may be used if bovine material is not available. Bungs and bladders are generally packed salted or dried and should be soaked overnight in cold water (5-7°C) in a cold room. The casings should be removed from the cold room one to two hours before they are to be used, and soaked in lukewarm water.

The sausage meat should be machine or hand-stuffed as firmly as possible in the bladders. These must then be pricked with a needle pad to allow entrapped air to escape from under the casing. The sausage should be tied off with heavy twine which may be passed lengthways around the product if desired.

Ripening and cooking

The sausage should be spaced carefully on smoke sticks to prevent contact, and held in a room for 24 to 48 hours at 20°C to 22°C and a relative humidity of 75 to 80 per cent. This allows the casing to dry and develop an attractive colour. Mortadella sausages are not smoked. They are steam-cooked in a smokehouse at temperatures between 65°C and 68°C until the internal sausage temperature has reached 60°C. Care must be taken to ensure adequate air movement in the smokehouse (relative humidity of 65-70 per cent).

Packaging and storage

After cooking, the sausages are cooled in air to room temperature. They are then immersed in boiling water for 1 second to tighten the casing around the product.

Mortadella sausages should be individually wrapped in cheesecloth bags and held at 11°C to 15°C (relative humidity of 65 to 75 per cent) until the product has lost approximately 20 per cent of its weight (two to three days). The shelf life of the product will be improved if it is held under refrigeration throughout storage and marketing.

The complete production sequence is illustrated in figure IV.6.

IV. FRANKFURTERS

Frankfurters are one of the most popular of all sausage products. They may be made from all beef, all pork or any combination of beef and pork. The

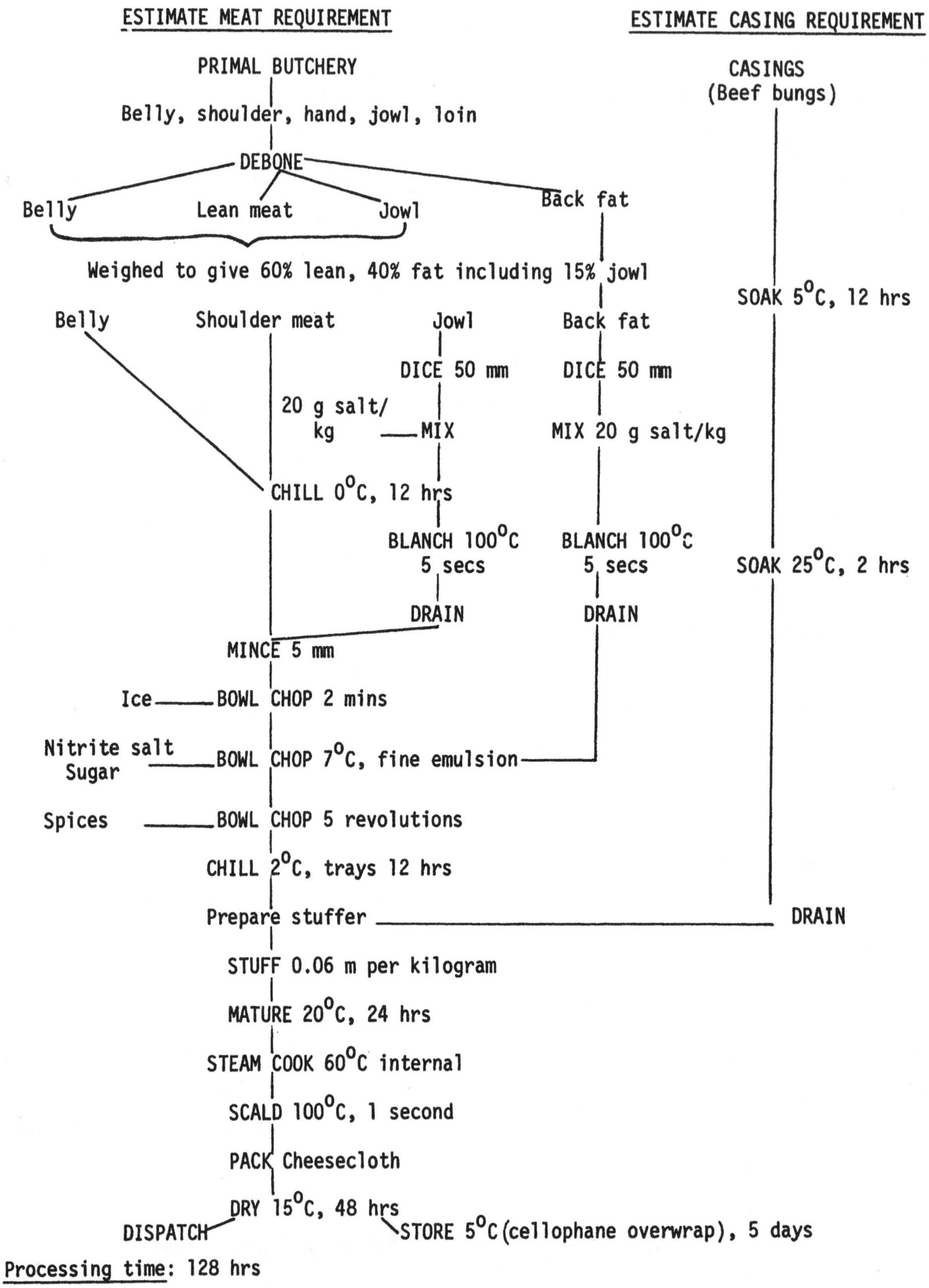

ESTIMATE MEAT REQUIREMENT   ESTIMATE CASING REQUIREMENT

PRIMAL BUTCHERY   CASINGS
                                                   (Beef bungs)
Belly, shoulder, hand, jowl, loin

DEBONE

Belly   Lean meat   Jowl   Back fat

Weighed to give 60% lean, 40% fat including 15% jowl

Belly   Shoulder meat   Jowl   Back fat   SOAK 5^{0}C, 12 hrs

                              DICE 50 mm   DICE 50 mm

20 g salt/
    kg   MIX   MIX 20 g salt/kg

CHILL 0^{0}C, 12 hrs

                        BLANCH 100^{0}C   BLANCH 100^{0}C
                           5 secs   5 secs   SOAK 25^{0}C, 2 hrs

                           DRAIN   DRAIN

MINCE 5 mm

Ice ———— BOWL CHOP 2 mins

Nitrite salt
Sugar ———— BOWL CHOP 7^{0}C, fine emulsion

Spices ———— BOWL CHOP 5 revolutions

CHILL 2^{0}C, trays 12 hrs

Prepare stuffer ————————————————————— DRAIN

STUFF 0.06 m per kilogram

MATURE 20^{0}C, 24 hrs

STEAM COOK 60^{0}C internal

SCALD 100^{0}C, 1 second

PACK Cheesecloth

DRY 15^{0}C, 48 hrs
DISPATCH   STORE 5^{0}C (cellophane overwrap), 5 days

Processing time: 128 hrs

Figure IV.6
Flow diagram illustrating the preparation of mortadella

manufacture of frankfurters is typical of the production of most fine-cut sausages stuffed into narrow casings. They are encased, linked, smoked and cooked and may be sold skinless or in their casings depending upon local taste.

IV.1 Ingredients

Frankfurters are made from fresh, uncured meat. For the production of high-quality, all pork products, it is usual to use only meat cuts from the shoulder and leg regions, although trimmed meat from the neck may also be included. The lean pork back fat and pork trimmings should be chilled prior to processing.

Table IV.4

Ingredients for the production of frankfurters

Ingredients	Quantity of ingredients per batch	Percentage of each ingredient
A. High quality frankfurters		
Lean pork	12.0 kg	54.87
Pork back fat	8.0 kg	36.58
Ice	1.4 kg	6.40
Nitrite salt	400 g	1.83
Ground white pepper	40 g	
Ground mace	20 g	0.32
Ground ginger	4 g	
Ground coriander	4 g	
Powdered lemon peel	2 g	
Casing required (narrow)	75 m	
Total ingredients (less casing)	21.87 kg	100.00

Yield on finished product = 95 per cent of recipe ingredients
Estimated carcase cut-out of meat inputs = 90 per cent
Carcase meat "bone-in" required: $20 \div 0.9 = 22.22$ kg
Yield on carcase meat "bone-in" = $(21.87 \div 22.22) \times 0.95 = 94$ per cent

Ingredients	Quantity of ingredients per batch	Percentage of each ingredient
B. Low quality frankfurters		
Lean pork	9.0 kg	32.92
Regular trimmings	7.0 kg	25.60
Pork fat	4.0 kg	14.63
Ice	5.9 kg	21.58
Dry skim milk powder	786 g	2.87
Nitrite salt	590 g	2.15
Ground white pepper	47 g	
Ground nutmeg	12 g	0.25
Garlic powder	3 g	
Casing required (narrow)	75 m	
Total ingredients (less casing)	27.34 kg	100.00

Yield on finished product = 95 per cent of recipe ingredients
Estimated carcase cut-out of meat ingredients: 92 per cent
Carcase meat "bone-in" required= $20 \div 0.92 = 21.74$ kg
Yield on carcase meat "bone-in" = $(27.34 \div 21.74) \times 0.95 = 119$ per cent

Figure IV.7 shows first- and second-choice meat cuts used in the production of Frankfurters while table IV. 4 provides the quantities of ingredients needed for a given batch of high- and low-quality products.

IV.2 Processing stages

Mincing

The lean meat and fat should be minced separately through a 4-mm plate.

Chopping

After the meat has been minced, it should be placed in the cutter with the nitrite salt, seasonings and one-quarter of the ice and chopped for several revolutions. It is necessary to restrict ice addition at this stage to ensure maximum extraction of the salt-soluble contractile proteins which improve the binding of the finished product. Finally, the fat and the remainder of the ice is added and chopped until the temperature reaches 15°C. Temperature, rather than time, is a better guide in chopping. Other ingredients, such as non-meat proteins (cereals, milk powder) are added during the final ice addition stage since they will readily absorb water and interfere with the extraction of soluble meat protein.

Stuffing

Small cellulose or sheep casings are generally used in the manufacture of frankfurters, but small hog casings may be used as an alternative.

Cellulose casings give the sausages a uniform diameter and length and the ability to withstand modern, high temperature, rapid processing conditions. They are easy to stuff, possess a high degree of resilience to breakage and are permeable to smoke when moist. Small cellulose casings are manufactured in lengths of 20-50 metres with stuffed diametres of 15-30 mm.

Sheep casings are usually sold in 100 metre hanks and graded according to stuffed diameter, which may range from 16 mm to 27 mm. According to grade, 10 kg of chopped meat should fill between 33 and 60 metres of casings. They should be soaked at 25°C for two hours before use.

Small hog casings have a larger stuffed diameter than sheep or cellulose casings. Only the narrow or medium grades should be used for the manufacture of frankfurters. Approximately 20 metres of casings are required for the manufacture of 10 kg of sausage.

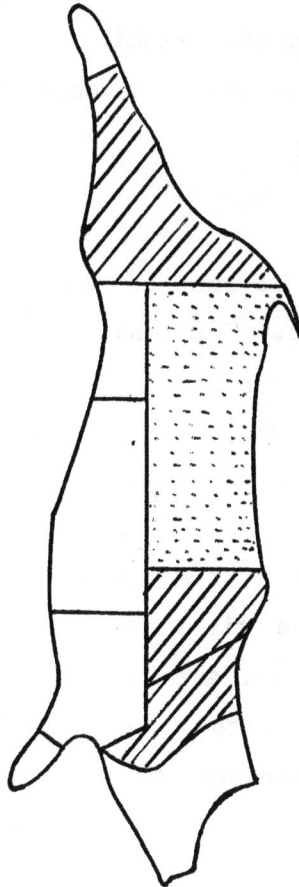

//// First choice

Second choice

Figure IV.7

Frankfurter materials

Salted hog or sheep casings should be flushed with water prior to being placed on the stuffing horn. Excess water is removed during stuffing by stripping between the fingers. As the casing fills it should be held firmly between the fingers to eliminate air pockets.

Linking

As the casing fills, it should be allowed to work off the stuffing horn on to a table. The tube of sausage meat may be divided into lengths of 12-15 cm either by manual linking or by automatic linking machines. Although machines are time-saving, they are expensive and can only really be justified for capacities in excess of 250 kg/hour.

Smoking and cooking

After the sausage is linked, it is hung on smoking sticks and sprayed with cold water to wash off adhering meat. The links on the stick should not touch each other.

Smoking times and temperatures vary considerably according to plant facilities. A simple smoking and cooking cycle lasts for two-and-a-half to three hours, during which time the centre sausage temperature is raised to 68°C. Smoke is applied during the first 30 minutes to produce desirable surface colour and develop the surface skin. The temperature of the smokehouse should be held at 60°C, with a relative humidity of 40 per cent during the smoking stage. After smoking, the temperature is raised to 80°C for final cooking.

When animal casings are used, the initial smoking is preceded by drying of the sausage surface. This is important in providing a surface to which smoke will adhere rather than penetrate.

Chilling

Frankfurters should be chilled immediately after cooking to an internal temperature of 30°C. This causes the sausage to swell slightly and improves its appearance. Spraying with cold water is particularly effective. After chilling, the sausages should be held in a cold store to cool further and dry. Excessive removal of moisture from the product should be avoided.

Packaging and storage

Frankfurters may be stored and sold unwrapped provided they are chilled. The shelf life of the unwrapped, fresh product is no longer than five days, after which the skin will shrivel and the flavour will become rancid. If

The complete production sequence is illustrated in figure IV.8.

V. COOKED HAM

Cooked ham is a cured, moulded and fully cooked pork product which may be sold whole or sliced and packaged.

V.1 Ingredients

Cooked ham, traditionally prepared from the hind leg of the pig, is now also prepared from the foreleg and shoulder cuts. These may be cured as a whole side and detached subsequently for cooking, or may be excised and cured separately. The hind and foreleg cuts should not be deboned prior to cooking but should be skinned and partially defatted.

Figure IV.9 shows first- and second-choice cuts for the preparation of cooked ham while table IV.5 gives the composition of the pumping and cover brines.

Table IV.5
Pumping and immersion brine composition for cooked ham

Ingredients	Quantities per batch of brine[1]
A. Pumping brine:	
Salt	6 kg
Sodium nitrite	30 g
Sodium nitrate	60 g
Sugar (sucrose)	60 g
Potable water	20 litres
B. Immersion brine	
Salt	12 kg
Sodium nitrite	72 g
Sodium nitrate	120g
Sugar (sucrose)	120 g
Potable water	40 litres

Yield on finished product = 94 per cent of meat ingredients
Estimated carcase cut-out trimmed leg= 80 per cent
Carcase meat "bone-in" required for 10 kg finished product : $(10 \div 0.94 \quad 0.8$
$$= 13.3 \text{ kg}$$
Yield on carcase meat "bone-in" : $(10 \div 13.3) = 75$ per cent.
[1] The amount of pumping and immersion brine necessary per unit of meat are discussed later in this section.

Processing stages

Curing

Curing includes muscle pumping and brine soaking. These two operations

ESTIMATE MEAT REQUIREMENT   ESTIMATE CASING REQUIREMENT

PRIMAL BUTCHERY   CASINGS (sheep narrow)

Shoulder, neck, lean trimmings

DEBONE

Lean   Fat   Back fat

Weighed to give 55% lean and 45% fat

Lean meat   Fat

MINCE 4 mm   CHILL

Nitrite salt⎫
25% ice   ⎬— BOWL CHOP 5 revolutions   MINCE 4 mm
Seasoning ⎭

75% ice ——— BOWL CHOP fine emulsion 15°C
(non-meat
protein if used)

Prepare stuffer————————————— SOAK 25°C, 2 hrs

STUFF 4m per kilogram

LINK 50-100 g portion 12-15 cm

SMOKE 60°C, 30 mins

COOK 80°C, internal

SPRAY COOL 30°C internal

DRY 0°C, 24 hrs

DISPATCH   STORE

0°C, cellophane, 5 days   0°C, vacuum pack, 5 weeks

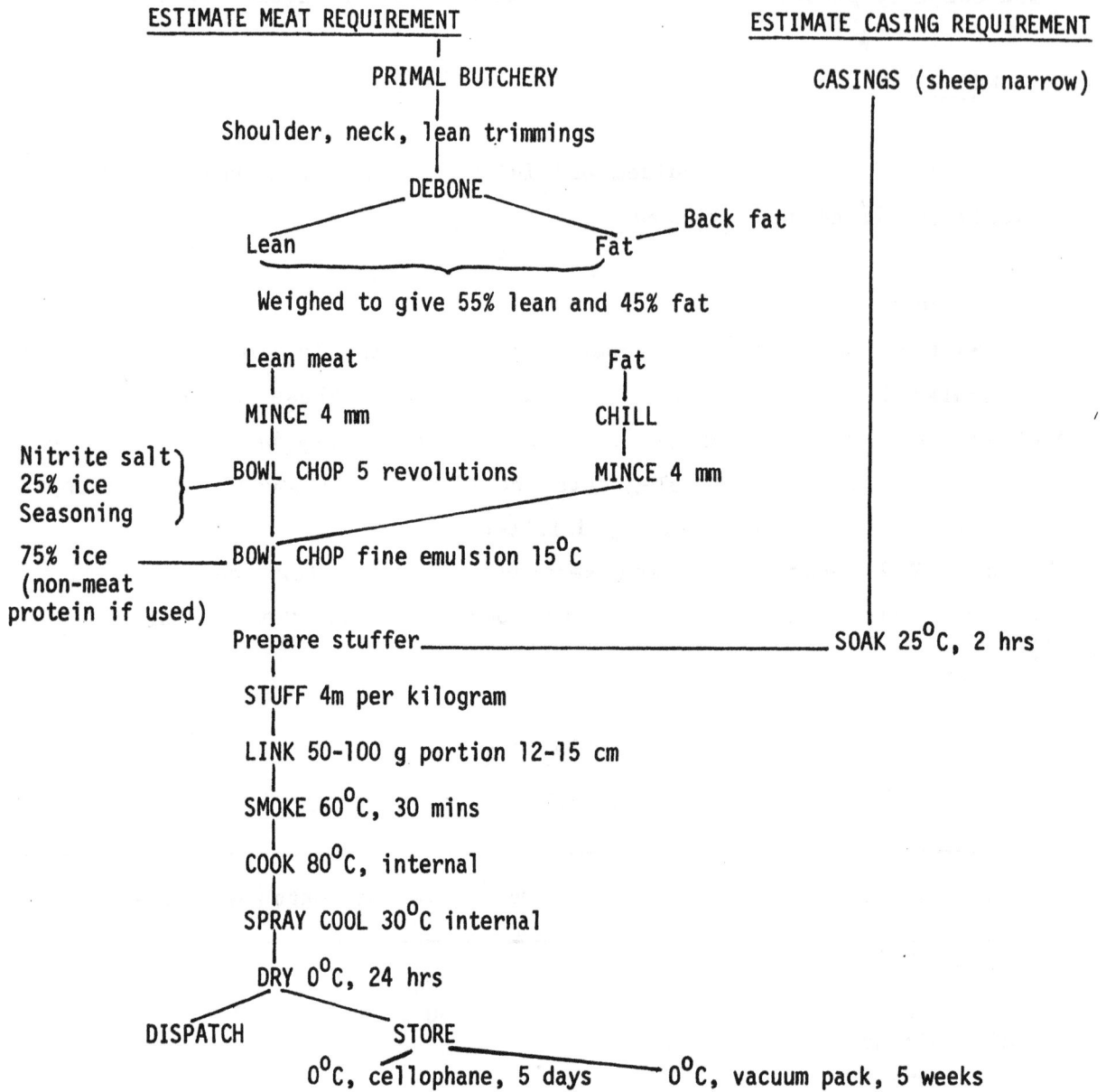

Processing time: 48 hrs

Figure IV.8

Flow diagram for the preparation of
frankfurter sausage

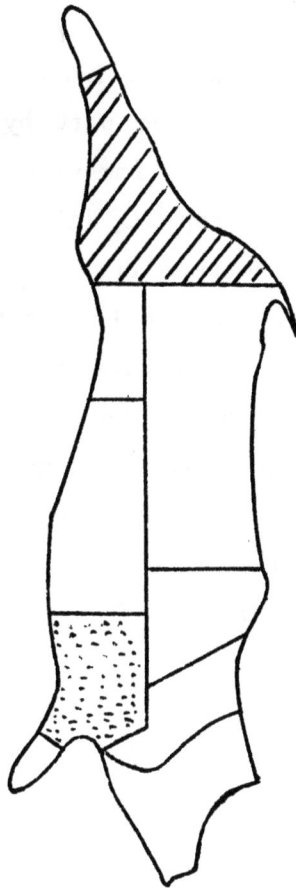

//// First choice

.·.· Second choice

Figure IV.9

Cooked ham materials

(i)   <u>Muscle pumping</u>: The object of the curing process is to distribute the curing ingredients uniformly throughout the meat. Among the main methods in use, muscle pumping is recommended for bone-in shoulders and ham. Refrigerated pumping brine (7°C) may be injected into the muscle via a hollow needle that has a number of holes along its length (see figure IV.10). Equipment is available with several needles which introduce the brine at several points at the same time. The equivalent of 8-10 per cent of the weight of the meat in brine should be injected, as quickly as possible, into the muscle at several sites.

(ii)   <u>Brine soaking</u>: After muscle pumping, the hams are immersed in the cover brine, using the proportion of one part by weight of meat to two parts by weight of brine. Complete immersion may be achieved by resting a weight on the ham to keep it under the surface. Hams should remain in the brine for between one and one-and-a-half days per kg of product weight. Thus, for a 6 kg ham the total immersion time is six to nine days. The temperature of the brine should be maintained at 5°C and must never be allowed to exceed 8°C. It is not recommended to reuse the brine. Its strength will be reduced by the uptake of curing agents into the meat and through dilution with meat juices. The brine may also become contaminated. The han should then be drained for two hours at 2°C.

Maturation

After curing, the hams and shoulders should be hung in a refrigerated room (4°-7°C) for 10-12 days to mature.

Deboning and moulding

After maturation, the hams and shoulders must be washed in warm water to remove surface deposits of salt and then hung to dry (eight to 12 hours at 6°C). When dry, they should be carefully deboned, avoiding unnecessary cuts in the meat.

Each deboned ham or shoulder should be weighed and pieces of similar weight separated so that they may be cooked together. Individual hams should then be placed in metal moulds called presses (see figure IV.11). Stainless steel is preferred because of its resistance to corrosion and its tensile strength. After the ham has been placed in the mould, the press cover should be engaged on to the ratchets at the end of the mould and closed by forcing the spring loaded cover on to the ham. The fat side of the ham should be

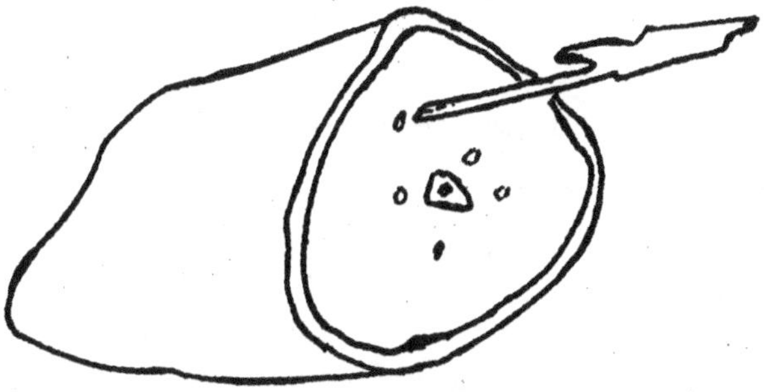

Figure IV.10

Muscle pumping of ham

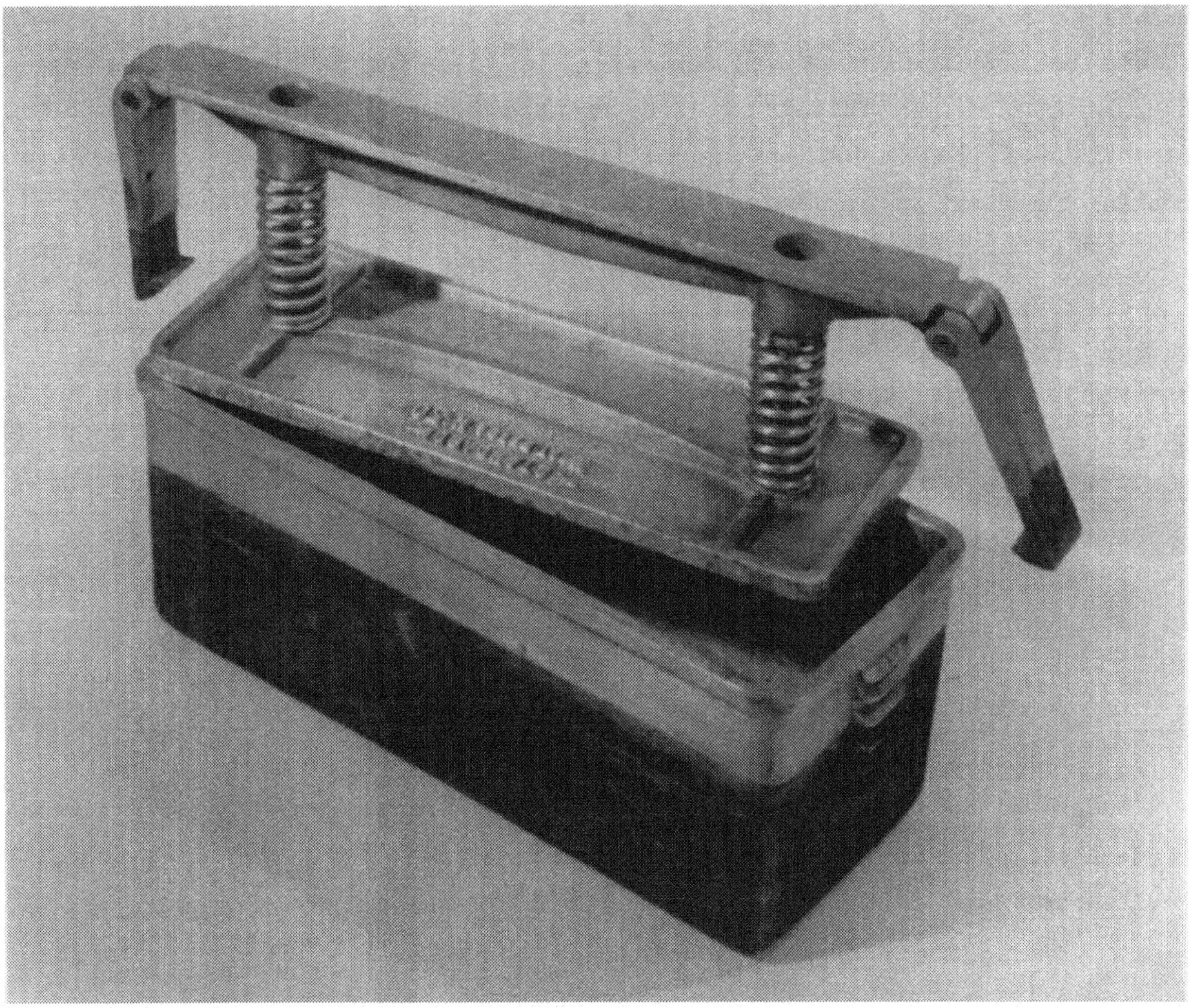

Figure IV.11

Ham mould

Parchment paper may be used to line the press to protect the ham from surface discolouration and to improve shape and appearance. Cotton stockinettes may be used as an alternative.

Cooking

In many parts of the world hams are smoked before cooking. If this operation is desired it should be carried out prior to deboning and moulding. Smoking at 20-24°C for two to four hours should be sufficient to produce the desired flavour and colour.

Hams may be cooked by steaming or by immersion in hot water. The latter method is favoured because it results in less product shrinkage. The moulds should be completely immersed in water at 65°C for one hour. The water temperature is then raised to 78°C and the hams cooked for various times depending on the weight and nature of the product. Some guide-lines for cooking times are as follows.

Leg		Shoulder	
Weight (kg)	Cooking time (78°C) in hours	Weight (kg)	Cooking time (78°C) in hours
2	2	2	1.5
4	3.5	3	3.0
5	4.5	4	4.0
6	5.5		

Shoulder hams are usually cooked for longer periods to improve tenderness. Time schedules such as those provided above will give internal ham temperatures of 66°C in the leg and 71°C in the shoulder.

Packaging and storage

After cooking, the moulds must be refrigerated for one day at 2°C. The ham should then be carefully removed and packaged. Unhygienic handling at this stage will increase surface contamination and reduce subsequent shelf-life.

Vacuum packing in cryovac bags is a commonly used method of packaging boneless ham. It provides a good barrier to contamination and reduces discoloration and weight loss due to evaporation. During storage and marketing, cooked hams must be held under refrigeration.

The complete production sequence is illustrated in figure IV.12.

VI. COOKED HAM (COMMINUTED)

New patented processes have been developed for the production of "whole ham" from individual pieces of cured meat. This product has a higher water content and is of a 'milder cure' than a traditional ham. Consequently, it also has a limited shelf life, both microbiologically and in appearance, and must be held at 0°C during retailing.

VI.1 Ingredients

Loin, blade and, to a certain extent, hand primal cuts are used, and are deboned initially as whole muscle blocks. Fat, skin and gristle are removed, with any trimmings diverted to fresh sausage production. For lower quality products, up to 10 per cent trimmed belly can be included.

Figure IV.13 shows first- and second-choice cuts for the preparation of comminuted cooked ham while table IV.6 gives the composition of pumping, cover and tumble brines.

VI.2 Processing stages

Curing

Curing involves muscle pumping and brine soaking. These two operations are briefly described below.

(i) Muscle pumping: All intact muscles are pumped to 110 per cent of their original weight with refrigerated brine. A multi-needle injector at 10 cm stages along the muscle block may be used for this purpose.

(ii) Brine soaking: To improve product binding, whole blocks should be immersed in a covering brine (one part meat, one part brine at 5°C for 24 hours). This stage is essentially an equilibration process and can be omitted if an automatic multi-needle injector machine is used, since the latter has a greater pumping efficiency.

- 78 -

ESTIMATE MEAT REQUIREMENT   ESTIMATE BRINE REQUIREMENT

PRIMAL BUTCHERY   PUMP BRINE   COVER BRINE

Shoulder   Leg   MIX   Salt
DEBONE   DISSOLVE Sodium nitrate
         Trimmings   Sodium nitrite
                                             Sucrose   MIX
PUMP TO 110% of original weight ——— COOL   Water   DISSOLVE
                                   7°C, 24 hrs
                                                          COOL 5°C, 24 hrs
IMMERSE 5°C, 6-9 days

(1 - 1½ days per kg weight)

DRAIN 2°C, 2 hrs

MATURE 4-7°C, 12 days

WASH IN WARM WATER

DRY 8-12 hrs, 6°C

OPTIONAL SMOKING (2-4 hrs, 20-24°C)

DEBONE LEG

Trimmings to   WEIGH
cured sausage

MOULD

COOK Leg 66°C internal

      Shoulder 71°C internal

COOL 2°C, 24 hrs

REMOVE MOULD

VACUUM PACK (Cryovac film)

DISPATCH 0°C   STORE 0°C, 5 days

Processing time: 20 days

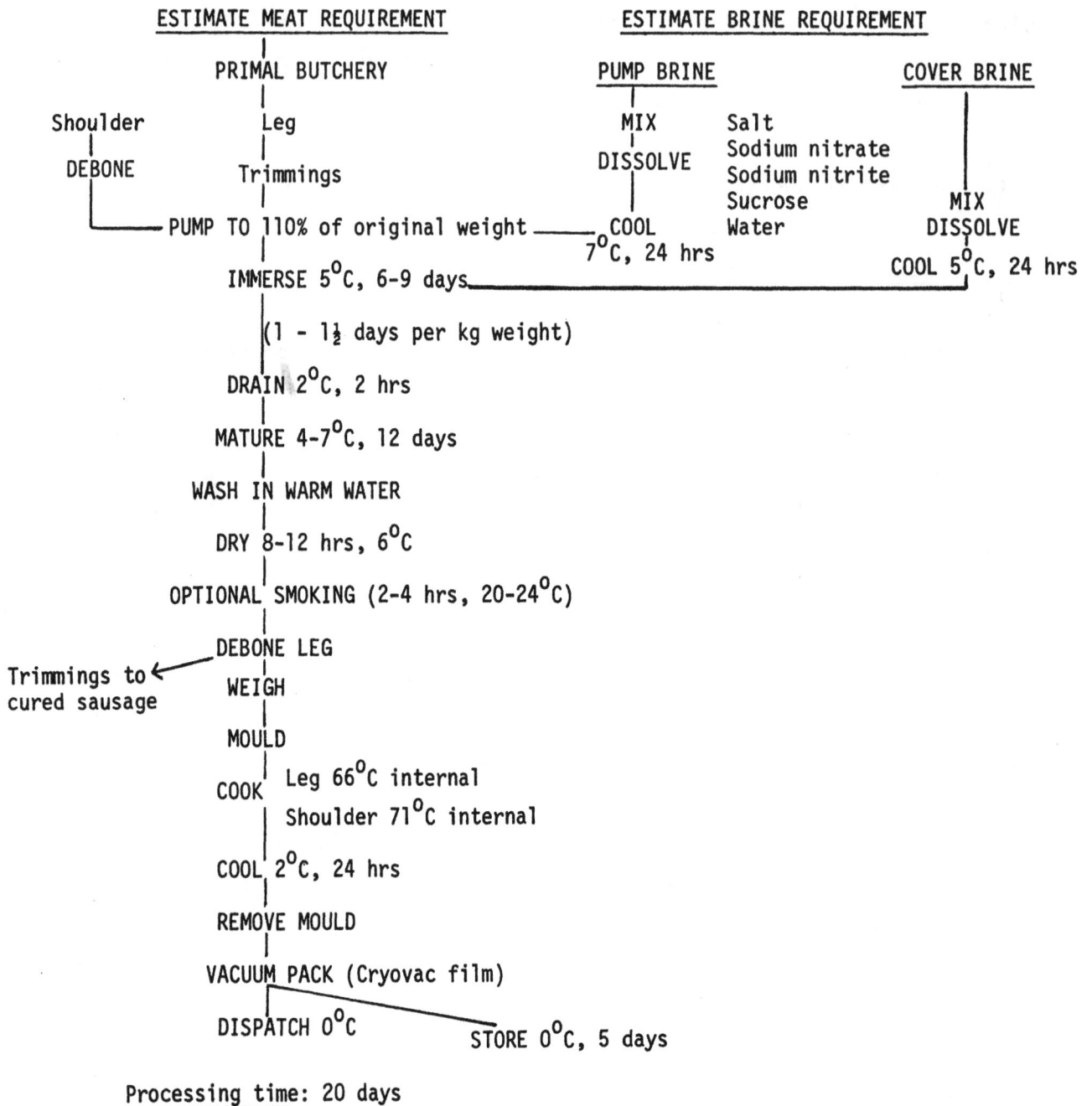

Figure IV.12
Diagram illustrating the preparation of cooked ham

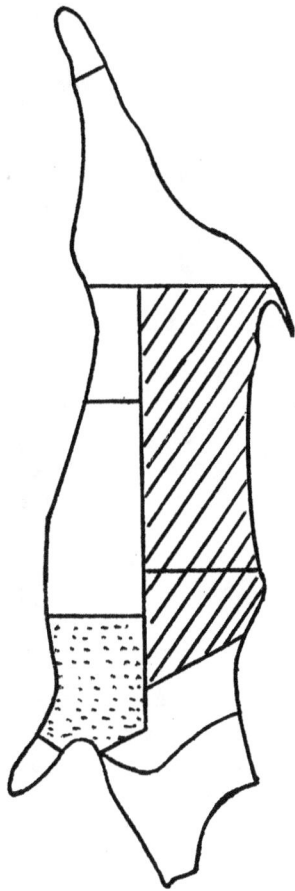

/// First choice

Second choice

<u>Figure IV.13</u>

<u>Cooked ham (comminuted) materials</u>

Table IV.6
Pumping, cover and tumble brine composition
for comminuted ham

Ingredients	Quantities per batch of brine[1]
A. Pumping brine	
Salt	3.75 kg
Sugar	415 g
Sodium pyrophosphate	1.25 kg
Sodium nitrate	46 g
Sodium nitrite	41 g
Potable water	20 litres
B. Cover brine	
Salt	7.5 kg
Sugar	830 g
Sodium pyrophosphate	2.5 kg
Sodium Nitrate	85 g
Sodium nitrite	85 g
Potable water	40 litres
C. Tumble brine	
Salt	700 g
Sugar	75 g
Sodium pyrophosphate	230 g
Sodium nitrate	7.5 g
Sodium nitrite	8.4 g
Potable water	20 litres

Yield on finished product = 100 per cent on meat ingredients
Estimated carcase cut-out of meat inputs= 90 per cent
Carcase meat "bone-in" required for 10 kg finished product: 10 0.9 = 11.11kg
Yield on carcase meat "bone-in" : 10: 11.11 = 90 per cent
[1] The amount of pumping and immersion brine necessary per unit of meat are discussed later in this section.

Tumbling

The meat is removed from the cover brine and allowed to drain. The muscle blocks are then reduced to homogeneous pieces weighing between 250 g and 1 kg, the size being dependent on the primal cut used. The pieces are placed in the tumbling machine with 10 per cent of their weight of tumbling brine. They should be tumbled for 8-15 minutes at 5°C or until the surface of the pieces becomes tacky.

Filling and moulding

Pieces are filled, often under pressure, into special cooking pack bags with a wide mouth stuffer. Pack sizes are usually 2.5 kg and 5 kg. Air is removed from the pack with a vacuum, polyclip closing machine or gentle tumbling machine makes the filling stage easier. The bags are placed in moulds and cooked by immersion in hot water. Cooking time depends upon the pack weight and should be continued until an internal temperature of 70°C is reached.

Packing and storage

After cooking, the moulds are left to equilibrate to ambient temperature and then refrigerated for one day at 2°C. The blocks are then removed and repacked into new vacuum pack bags for retail sale.

The complete production sequence is illustrated in figure IV.14.

VII. BACON

Bacon is prepared by curing cuts of partially deboned sides of pork and maturing under refrigeration to produce a product of distinctive colour and flavour. There are several methods of curing. The most common one is the Wiltshire cure, so called because it originated in England some 200 years ago. Bacon may be sold smoked or unsmoked ('green') and should be cooked immediately prior to being eaten.

VII.1 Ingredients

Bacon is usually prepared from 'heavy' pigs, having a live weight of between 90 and 100 kg. Excessively fatty pigs are not suitable. After splitting and before chilling, the backbone should be removed, care being taken not to cut into the underlying musculature. The exposed crest of aitch-bone should also be removed so that the remaining part of the bone does not protrude beyond the cushion of the gammon. The ribs should be carefully removed together with the skin or pleura of the rib cage. In some countries, a loop of string or cheese-wire is passed underneath the ribs and pulled from the top towards the belly, whilst thumb pressure is applied to the lifted end of the rib. This avoids unnecessary knife damage to underlying musculature. The oyster bones of the lower loin area should also be removed. This can be done without the use of a knife.

The pig's head should be excised so as to leave an even and unbroken cut surface at the fore end. Next the shoulder blade glands, blood clots and any discoloured fat around the blade socket should be trimmed and removed.

```
ESTIMATE MEAT REQUIREMENT              ESTIMATE BRINE REQUIREMENT
        |
PRIMAL BUTCHERY                  MUSCLE BRINE   COVER BRINE   TUMBLE BRINE
        |
Loin, blade                         MIX       Salt
        |                        DISSOLVE     Sodium nitrate
DEBONE                                        Sodium nitrite
        |                                     Sucrose
        |                                     Sodium polyphosphate
PUMP TO 110% original weight ———— COOL 5°C    Water
        |                                       |
IMMERSE 5°C, 24 hrs ———————————— COOL 5°C ——————— MIX            MIX
        |                                        DISSOLVE      DISSOLVE
DRAIN                                                            |
        |
WEIGH 250 g - 1 kg
        |
TUMBLE 5°C, 15 mins ————————————————————————————————————————— COOL 5°C
        |
VACUUM FILL (cook-pack bags)
        |
MOULD
        |
COOK 70°C internal
        |
COOL 2°C, 24 hrs
        |
DEBAG
        |
VACUUM PACK (Cryovac film)
        |
DISPATCH 0°C
```

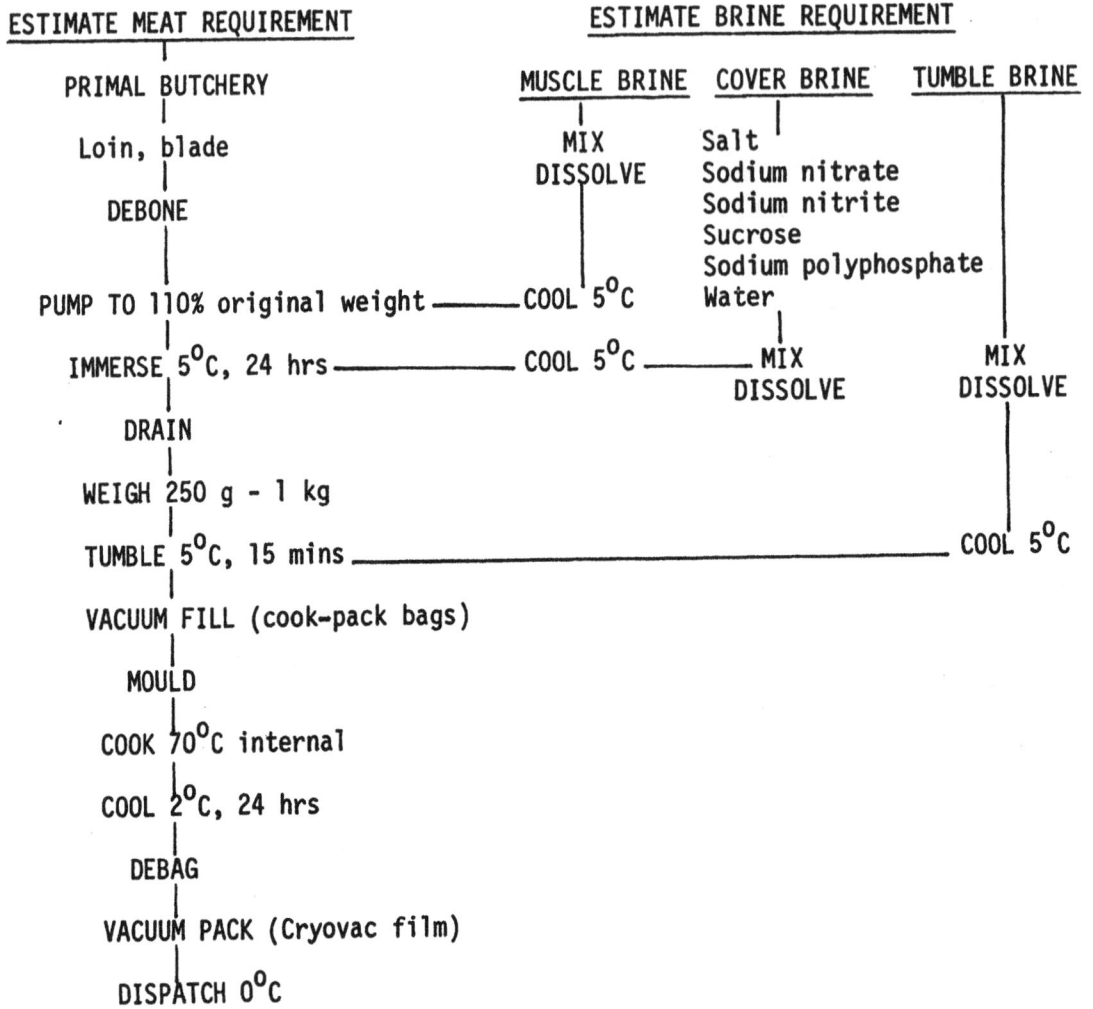

Processing time: 50 hrs

Figure IV.14
Diagram illustrating the preparation of
comminuted cooked ham

Finally, the fore-foot should be cut off at the upper point of the knee joint and the hind foot sawn off through the centre of the knee joint. After partial deboning, the carcases should be chilled at 2-4°C.

Figure IV.15 shows parts of the carcase used for the manufacture of bacon while table IV.7 provides the composition of the pumping and cover brines for 100 litres of water.

Table IV.7
Composition of pumping and cover brines
for the production of bacon

Ingredients	Quantities per batch of brine[1]
A. Pumping brine	
Salt 30 kg	
Potassium nitrate (salpetre)	3 kg
Sodium nitrite	50 g
Potable water	100 litres
B. Cover brine	
Salt 25 kg	
Potassium nitrate (saltpetre)	3 kg
Sodium nitrite	50 g
Potable water	100 litres

Yield on finished product = 95 per cent on deboned meat ingredients
Estimated carcase cut-out of meat input = 90 per cent
Carcase meat "bone-in" required for 10 kg output: $(10 \div 0.95) + 0.9 = 11.69$ kg
Yield on carcase meat "bone-in" : $10 + 11.69 = 85$ per cent
[1] The amount of pumping and immersion brine necessary per unit of meat are discussed later in this section.

VII.2 Processing stages
Pumping and curing

To accelerate the distribution of curing salts through the tissues, the sides should be injected with pumping brine. This should result in a weight increase of between 8 and 10 per cent. About 20 injection points, spaced so as to distribute the brine as evenly as possible through the lean meat, should be attempted. The shoulder cavity, left by the removal of the blade bone, should be packed with 100-150 g salt.

After pumping, the sides must be stacked in a brine tank with the skin downwards. Sufficient immersion or cover brine should then be added to cover

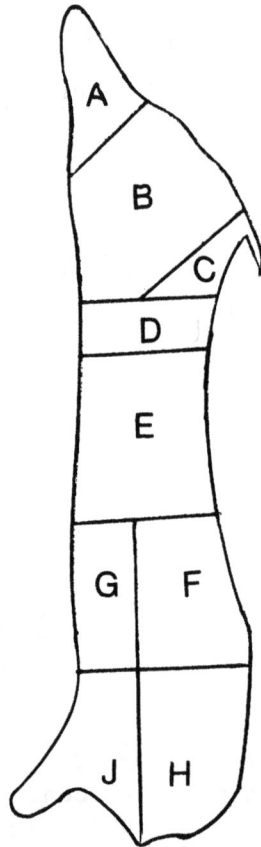

A. Gammon hack
B. Middle gammon
C. Corner gammon
D. Long back rasher
E. Middle or through cut rasher
F. Prime back rashers or chops
G. Prime streaky rashers
H. Prime collar
J. Prime forehock

Figure IV.15

Bacon materials

all the sides. These should be allowed to cure for four to five days at 4-5°C. Control of temperature is essential to ensure a high quality product. Cover brines should not be reused.

Maturation

After curing, the sides should be stacked, rind upwards, in piles not exceeding eight layers. They are then left to mature for seven days at 5-7°C.

Smoking and drying

If the bacon sides are to be sold smoked, they should be suspended in a smoke kiln in which smoke is generated by burning hardwood sawdust. Smoking should be carried out at 20°C until the product has acquired a golden yellow colour (5 to 8 hours). Smoking causes some drying of the sides. It also modifies the flavour and increases the shelf life of bacon. Unsmoked bacon is usually dried in warm air prior to marketing.

Packing and storage

Whole sides are packed in stockinettes (cheesecloth) and hung in a refrigerated chamber at 5°C. Weight loss should be of the order of 1 per cent per week. The sides are dispatched whole.

Retail preparation involves the cutting of each side into primal cuts as shown in figure IV.15 since bacon varies in quality depending on the location within the side. The primals are jointed or sliced. Once sliced, the product has a limited shelf-life (usually for two to five days at 0°C). Product shelf-life can be extended by vacuum packing or deep frozen storage in gas flushed vacuum packs.

The complete production sequence is illustrated in figure IV.16.

ESTIMATE MEAT REQUIREMENT   ESTIMATE BRINE REQUIREMENT
            | | |
       SPLIT CARCASE   PUMP BRINE   COVER BRINE
            | | |
         CHINE   Salt
            | Sodium nitrate
        REMOVE   Sodium nitrite
            | Water
Head, foot, H-bone, rib bone, blade bone
            | | |
 Fresh   TRIM SHOULDER   MIX   MIX
 sausage | DISSOLVE   DISSOLVE
         CHILL 2-4°C | |
            | | |
PUMP TO 108% original weight————————————COOL 5°C   COOL 5°C
            |
(Pack shoulder with salt)
       IMMERSE 5°C, 4-5 days——————————————————————————————
            |
         DRAIN
            |
MATURE 5°C, 7 days
            |
(SMOKE 20°C, 5-8 hrs)
            |
DRY 5°C, 24 hrs
            |————————————————
PACK Cheesecloth   PRIMAL BUTCHERY
       | |
DISPATCH 5°C   HOLD 5°C   JOINT   SLICES
                  10 days | |
                          PACK   PACK   PACK
                        Cellophane Vacuum Cellophane
                          | | |
                  DISPATCH HOLD 0°C DISPATCH DISPATCH HOLD 0°C,
                           5 days   3 days

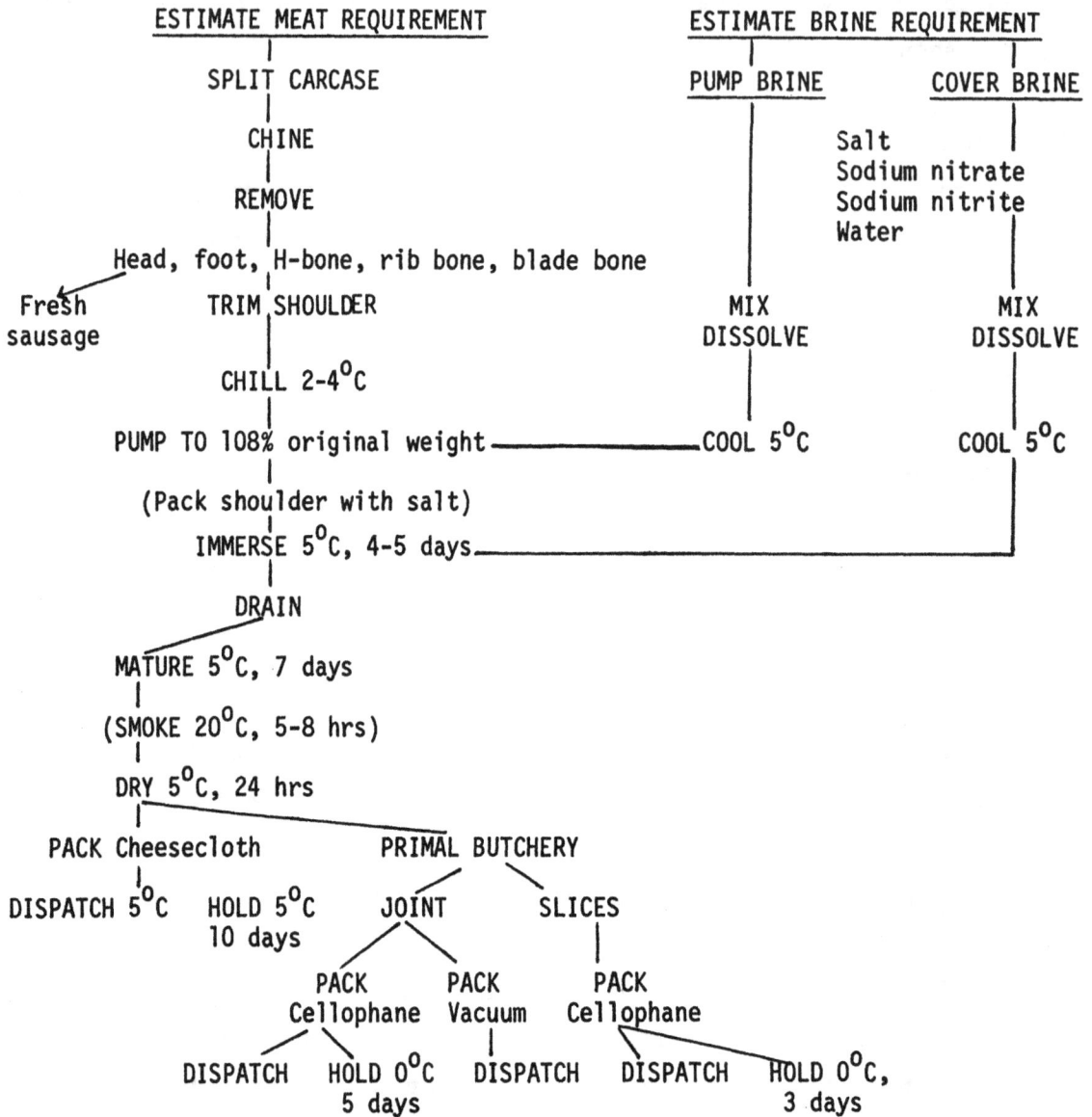

Processing time: 12 days

Figure IV.16

Flow diagram illustrating bacon preparation

CHAPTER V

EVALUATION OF ALTERNATIVE
MEAT PROCESSING TECHNIQUES

I. <u>INTRODUCTION</u>

The purpose of this chapter is to describe a simple evaluation methodology which may be used by practising or would-be meat processors for the evaluation of alternative processing techniques and scales of production. Section II describes the methodology in general terms while section III illustrates its application to the two production models described in Chapter III. Section IV analyses additional factors which should be taken into consideration when evaluating projects in this sector.

Findings from the evaluation of the production models described in section III do not necessarily appply to all situations and the reader is not advised to make investment decisions on the basis of these findings. The following three points should be borne in mind:

- the evaluations, though based on data from developing countries, are only intended to illustrate principles and methods. They do not indicate the financial viability or non-viability of the production methods under all possible conditions;

- because the provisions and effects of these models vary from country to country and with each individual situation, no account has been taken in the evaluation of taxation, eligibility for government subsidies or special measures favouring small-scale enterprises. These factors must be taken into account where appropriate; and

- it will be necessary for potential producers to calculate for themselves the capacities required (buildings, equipment, and so on) and the types and levels of operating inputs needed, according to market size and the product mix required.

A pork processing plant requires some or all of the following elements for its effective establishment and operation:

- a suitable site (e.g. in terms of closeness to raw materials and/or markets);
- a reliable external source of electricity or the capacity to generate it;
- a reliable source of treated water;
- qualified labour for some of the operations;
- managerial and technical expertise;
- reliable sources of raw materials; and
- a market for the product.

It is important that potental entrepreneurs check all the above elements prior to deciding whether to invest in any particular plant.
45The two production models evaluated in this chapter have the following characteristics:

Model 1: This plant is designed to produced 100 tonnes of pork products per annum, of which 25 tonnes are cooked ham, 60 tonnes mortadella and 15 tonnes fresh sausage. The plant employs nine workers and operates 250 working days per year (50 weeks), for eight hours per day (one shift). Average weekly production is therefore equal to 2 tonnes of products;

-Model 2: This plant is designed to produce 80 tonnes of pork products per annum, of which 68 tonnes are ham (32 tonnes of good quality cooked hindquarter and shoulder and 36 tonnes of lower-quality comminuted ham) and 12 tonnes are fresh sausage (made from the trimmings which are not suitable for the production of ham). The plant employs eight workers and operates 250 days per year for eight 8 hours per day.

In both models the following assumptions are made:
- that the plant is run as an entirely separate operation from the slaughterhouse or butchery business;

- that supplies of whole pig carcases are delivered for processing from a nearby slaughterhouse (all inputs are therefore of "bone-in" meat); and

- that a suitable system is available for distributing and retailing the finished pork products at additional costs (i.e. revenues are based on factory gate prices).

The evaluation is therefore concerned with production from the point where carcases are delivered to the plant to the point where the finished pork products leave the factory.

II. EVALUATION METHODOLOGY

The staff of financial institutions, businessmen and government officials may have their own evaluation methodology but may still find the one described in this memorandum useful, especially if they are unfamiliar with the processing of pork.

The evaluation framework consists of three main parts:

- the determination of quantities of various inputs used in the processing of pork (steps 1 to 5);
- the estimation of the cost of each input and that of unit production costs (steps 6 to 13); and
- the calculation of the project profitability (steps 14 and 15).

These steps are described below. Producers wishing to identify the most appropriate technique should repeat these steps for each technology which may yield the required output.

Step 1: Determination of the quantity and type of processed meat to be produced each year. These are a function of market demand, availability of investment funds, adopted production techniques, availability of raw materials and so on.

Step 2: Estimation of the quantities of the various materials inputs for the adopted scale of production and product mix. The main materials for pork processing are:

- pork meat (various cuts, trimmings);
- salt;
- sugar;
- nitrite and nitrate;
- spices;
- casings;
- water;
- packaging materials; and
- power (eletricity).

Step 3: Compilation of a list of required equipment, including spare parts and servicing and testing equipment. Both locally made and imported equipment should be included.

Step 4: Determination of labour requirements. It should be noted that the productivity of the labour force may be significantly different from one region to another. Labour requirements are dependent on the number of shift per day, working days per week, and working weeks per year. In addition, the number of workers should be specified for each skill level.

Step 5: Determination of the local infrastructure required. This may include:

- land for the plant; and
- buildings, including processing hall, storage areas, office and so on.

Step 6: Determination of the working capital required since operating costs would be incurred before revenues from sales are realised. In general, working capital is estimated at 25 per cent of annual operating costs (cost of materials plus that of labour).

Step 7: Determination of the annual depreciation costs of equipment and buildings. Whatever the type of equipment used, it will have a limited life (10 years). An estimate must thus be made of the annual equipment depreciation costs. The same applies to buildings which may be taken to have a life of 25 years. Depreciation costs are dependent on initial purchase price, the life of equipment and buildings and the prevailing interest rate. Table V.1 located at the end of this chapter, may be used to estimate these costs. It provides the annuity factor (F) for interest rates up to 40 per cent and expected life periods up to 25 years. For example, for an interest rate of 10 per cent and an expected life of five years, the annuity factor F is equal to 3.791. Thus, if Z is the purchase price of the equipment or cost of building, the annual depreciation cost is equal to Z/F. Hence the longer the useful life, the lower the annual depreciation cost, and the higher the prevailing interest rate, the higher the depreciation cost.

The c.i.f. prices of imported pieces of equipment may be obtained from local importers or equipment suppliers. The prices of local equipment and building may be obtained from local contractors and equipment manufacturers.

Step 8: Determination of the annual cost of land: land has an infinite life. Thus, the annual cost of land may be assumed to be equal to the annual rent of equivalent land.

Step 9: Calculation of the annual cost of materials identified in step 2.

Step 10: Calculation of the annual cost of labour. This cost varies greatly from one region to another and must be calculated on the basis of local wage rates. The labour requirements are those identified in step 4.

Step 11: Working capital raised for the project will require an allowance in the annual costs for interest payments to be made on this capital.

Step 12: The total annual production cost consists of the sum of the separate annual costs itemised in steps 7 to 11.

Total annual production cost = Depreciation cost of equipment and building + annual land rental cost + annual labour costs + annual cost of materials + annual interest payments on working capital.

Step 13: The average unit production cost for the adopted product mix is equal to:

Total annual cost : annual output

The unit production cost of any individual meat product may be estimated as follows:

(i)   calculate the sum of cost items estimated in steps 7, 8, 10 and 11;

(ii)   divide the above sum by the total number of tonnes of meat processed per year; this gives the unit production cost, excluding unit materials cost (from step 9);

(iii) estimate the total cost of materials (meat, spices, etc.) used in the manufacture of the meat product;

(iv)   estimate the unit materials cost by dividing the total materials costs by the number of tonnes produced each year, and;

(v)   add the unit materials cost to the unit cost estimated under (ii) above.

Step 14: Estimation of total revenues from sales on the basis of an estimate of wholesale or retail prices of the various meat products produced by the plant.

Step 15: Estimation of total profits before taxes. These are equal to total revenues minus total annual production costs.

III. APPLICATION OF THE EVALUATION METHODOLOGY

The evaluation methodology is applied to the two production models specified in the previous section.

III.1 Model 1: 100 tonnes per year meat processing plant

Step 1:
- Plant capacity : 100 tonnes/year
- Product mix: - 25 tonnes of cooked ham
              - 60 tonnes of mortadella
              - 15 tonnes of fresh sausage

Step 2: Yearly material inputs (estimated on the basis of data
        from Chapters III and IV):

- 93 -

- pig-meat   115 tonnes
- salt, nitrite salt   20 tonnes
- spices   434 kg
- other additives   293 kg
- sausage casings   40 km
- packaging materials   100 tonnes
- electricity   140,000 kW
- water   1.75 million litres

Step 3: List of required equipment, including life of each piece of
        equipment : see Appendix IV.

Step 4: Labour requirements

The plant operates one eight-hour shift per working day for a total of 250
working days per year. The personnel required include the following:

- 1 manager;
- 2 butchers;
- 3 processors;
- 2 processing assistants; and
- 1 unskilled worker;
Total number of staff: 9

Step 5: Land and building requirements.
- total land required : 2,000 m^2
- buildings required (see Chapter III for layout):

Item	Area (m^2)
Processing and butchery area	183
Cooking and smoking room	27
Packaging room	15
Office, toilets	15
Maintenance and boiler room (separate)	15
Cold storage modules	23
Concrete apron	45

Step 6: Working capital required is equal to three months operating costs
(for labour, materials and maintenance). This amounts to 25 per cent of the
cost items estimated in steps 7, 9 and 10 below:

(US$24,705 + US$216,970 + US$10,430) x 0.25 = US$63,038

Step 7: Annual depreciation costs of equipment and buildings

- Equipment: The interest rate used for the calculation of equipment depreciation costs is assumed to be 12 per cent. The lives of the various pieces of equipment are given in Appendix IV. The total cost of equipment with lives of 5, 10 and 15 years respectively is:

Cost of equipment (US$)	Useful life (years)	Discount factor (F)	Depreciation costs (US$)
35 110	5	3.605	9 739
52 160	10	5.650	9 232
61 300	15	6.811	9 000

Total annual depreciation cost of equipment: US$27 971

- Buildings: The total cost of buildings is estimated at US$59,950[1]. Their assumed useful life is 25 years. Thus, for a 12 per cent interest rate, the discount factor, F, is equal to 7.843. The buildings depreciation cost is then equal to:

$$US\$ \ 59,950 \ : \ 7.843 \ = \ US\$ \ 7,644$$

- The annual cost of spares and maintenance should be added to the annual equipment and buildings depreciation costs in order to obtain total annual depreciation costs. The latter is estimated at 5 per cent of the cost of equipment and buildings:

$$(148,570 + 59,950) \times 0.05 \ = \ US\$10,430$$

Thus, the total annual depreciation cost is equal to:

$$US\$ \ 27,971 \ + \ US\$7,644 + US\$10,430 \ = \ US\$46,045$$

---

[1] This estimate is based on the following unit costs:
- US$150 per m^2 for processing and butchery area, packaging room and maintenance and boiler rooms;
- US$200 per m^2 for cooking and smoking room;
- US$160 per m^2 for office and toilets;
- US$800 per m^2 for cold storage modules; and
- US$40 per m^2 for concrete apron.

Step 8: Annual rental cost of land. This is assumed to be equivalent to an interest of 12 per cent paid on the value of land:

- assumed value of the land: US$1,000
- annual rental cost = $1,000 x 0.12 = $120

Step 9: Annual cost of material inputs and other miscellaneous items:

Item	Unit cost ($)	Quantity	Total cost (US$)
Pig meat	1,400/tonne	115 tonnes	161 000
Salt, nitrite salt	130/tonne	20 tonnes	2 600
Spices	2,150/tonne	434 kg	930
Other additives	650/tonne	293 kg	190
Sausage casings	0.4/metre	40 km	16 000
Packaging	0.05/kg	100 T	5 000
Electricity	0.10/kW	140,000 kW	14 000
Water	1.30/1,000 litres	1.75 million litres	2 280
Insurance[1]			2 090
Knives, ham moulds, etc.[2]			1 180
Office expenses[2]			3 000
Detergents and cleaning utensils[2]			2 200
Sundries and unforeseen[2]			6 500
Total annual cost			216 970

Step 10: Annual labour costs

Category	Number	Cost (US$)
Manager	1	4 400
Butcher	2	6 600
Processor	3	8 250
Assistant processor	2	4 000
Labourer	1	1 500
Total	9	24 750

---

[1] Equal to 1 per cent of the value of buildings and equipment.

[2] Estimated.

Step 11: Annual cost of working capital at a 12 per cent interest rate:

US$63,038 x 0.12 = US$7.565

Step 12: Total annual production cost (sum of totals from steps 7-11):

US46,045 + US120 + US216,970 + US24,750 + US7,565 = US$295,450

Step 13: Production cost per average tonne of product:

US295,450   100 tonnes = US$2,954.5/tonne

Step 14: Annual revenue from sale of output:

Product	Quantity (tonnes)	Price, ex-plant per tonne (US$)	Annual revenue (US$)
Ham, cooked	25	4 000	100 000
Mortadella	60	3 500	210 000
Fresh sausage (uncooked, unsmoked)	15	2 100	31 500
Total	100		341 500

Step 15: Annual profits before taxes:

US$341,500 - US$295,450 = US$46,050

III.2 Model 2: 80 tonnes per year meat processing plant

Step 1: The plant has the capacity to produce 80 tonnes of pork products per annum with the following product mix:

- 65 tonnes ham (32 tonnes good quality, 36 tonnes lower quality);
- 12 tonnes fresh sausage.

Step 2: Yearly material inputs (estimated on the basis of data from Chapters III and IV).

- pig-meat   95 tonnes
- salt, nitrite salt   35 tonnes
- spices   68 kg
- other additives   1,350 kg
- sausage casings   24 km
- packaging materials   80 tonnes
- electricity   185,000 kW
- water   1.75 million litres

Step 3: List of equipment required: see Appendix IV.

Step 4: Labour requirements.

The plant operates one eight-hour shift per working day for a total of 250 working days per annum. The personnel required includes the following:
- manager   1
- butcher   3
- processor   2
- processing assistant 1
- labourer   <u>1</u>
- Total   8

Step 5: Land and building requirements

Total land required: 2,000 m^2
Buildings required (see Chapter III for layout)

Item	Area (m^2)
Processing and butchery area	183
Cooking and smoking room	27
Packaging room	15
Office, toilets	15
Maintenance and boiler room (separate)	15
Cold storage modules	25
Concrete apron	45

Step 6: Working capital required is equal to three months operating costs (for maintenance, materials and labour). This amounts to 25 per cent of the sum of cost items estimated in steps 7, 9 and 10 below:

(US$10,432 + US$23,300 + US$184,980) x 0.25 = <u>US$54,678</u>

Step 7: Annual depreciation costs of equipment and buildings.
- Equipment: The interest rate used for the calculation of equipment depreciation costs is assumed to be 12 per cent. The lives of the various pieces of equipment are given in Appendix IV. The total cost of equipment with lives of respectively 5, 10 and 15 years respectively is as follows:

Cost of equipment	Useful life (years)	Annuity factor(F)	Depreciation cost (US$)
35 110	5	3.605	9 739
38 120	10	5.650	6 747
73 870	15	6.811	10 846
Total annual depreciation cost of equipment:			27 332

- Buildings:

Assumed useful life = 25 years. Interest rate = 12 per cent.

The total cost of buildings is assumed to be US$61,550.[1] The annuity factor (F) is equal to 7.843. The buildings annual depreciation cost is then equal to:

$$US\$61,550 \quad 7.843 = US\$7,848$$

- The annual cost of spares and maintenance should be added to the annual equipment and building depreciation costs in order to obtain the total annual depreciation costs. The latter is estimated at 5 per cent of the cost of equipment and buildings:

$$(147,100 + 61,550) \times 0.05 = US\$10,432$$

Thus, total annual depreciation cost is equal to:

$$US\$27,332 + US\$7,848 \ 1 \ US\$10,432 = US\$45,612$$

Step 8: Annual rental cost of land. This is assumed to be equivalent to an interest rate of 12 per cent paid on the value of the land:

- assumed land value: US$1,000
- annual rental cost: 1,000 x 0.12 = US$120

Step 9: Annual cost of material inputs and other miscellaneous items:

Item	Unit cost($)	Quantity	Total cost(US$)
Pig-meat	1,400/tonne	95 tonnes	133 000
Salt, nitrite salt	130/tonne	35 tonnes	4 550
Spices	2,150/tonne	68 kg	150
Other additives	650/tonne	1.35 tonnes	880
Sausage casings	0.3/metre	24 km	7 200
Packaging	50/tonne	80 tonnes	4 000

[1] The total cost of buildings is estimated on the basis of the unit costs used for Model 1 (see note on p. 94).

Electricity	0.1/kW	185,000 kW	18 500
Water	1.3/1,000 litres	1.75 million litres	2 280
Insurance[1]			2 090
Knives, ham moulds, etc.[2]			1 830
Office expenses[2]			2 500
Detergents and cleaning utensils[2]			2 000
Sundries and unforeseen			6 000
Total annual costs			184 980

Step 10 : Annual labour costs

Category	Number	Cost (US$)
Manager	1	4 400
Butcher	3	9 900
Processor	2	5 500
Processing assistant	1	2 000
Labourer	1	1 500
Total	8	23 300

Step 11: Annual cost of working capital at 12 per cent interest rate:

$$US\$54,678 \times 0.12 = US\$6,561$$

Step 12: Total annual production cost (sum of totals from steps 7-11):

$$US\$45,612 + US\$120 + US\$184,980 + US\$23,300 + US\$6,561 = US\$260,573$$

Step 13: Production cost per average tonne of product:

$$US\$ 260,573 \ 80 \text{ tonnes} = US\$3,257/Tonne$$

Step 14: Annual revenue from sale of output:

---

[1] Equal to 1 per cent of the value of buildings and equipment.

[2] Estimated.

Product	Quantity (tonnes)	Price, ex-plant per tonne (US$)	Annual revenue (US$)
Ham, cooked	32	4 000	128 000
Ham, comminuted	36	3 200	115 200
Fresh sausage	12	2 100	25 200
Total	80		268 400

Step 15: Annual profits before taxes:

US$268,400 - US$260,573 = US$7,827

IV.   OTHER CONSIDERATIONS IN PROJECT EVALUATION

IV.1 Sensitivity analysis

Any project evaluation makes use of various assumptions regarding the prices of raw materials, the retail prices of the output, the interest rate and so on. It is not certain that these assumptions will actually prevail after the start of the project. It is therefore advisable to repeat the evaluation with alternative · sets of "pessimistic" assumptions (e.g., higher prices of raw materials and equipment, higher interest rates, lower retail prices of the output). The entrepreneur may then have an idea of the risk he will be taking by investing in a given project. It is, in particular, important to repeat the evaluation for various pig-meat prices since the cost of meat inputs is by far the most important cost item. Entrepreneurs will then be able to know the maximum price they may afford to pay for raw meat while still making a profit.

IV.2 Choice of product and product price

The profitability of a meat processing plant will also depend on the choice of product mix and prevailing retail prices, the latter being a function of demand and supply conditions. For example, if markets for several alternative product mixes are available in a country, it would probably be worthwhile analysing several production models in order to identify the most profitable one.

Before returns from sales of pork products can be estimated, wholesale (ex-factory) prices must be known. In some countries, imported or domestically-produced pork products may already be on the market. Retail prices will then be available for these, although they may have to be adjusted if differences in quality are being considered or if the supply of meat products is to be increased substantially. In any case, ex-factory prices could be estimated from these retail prices by deducting retail and distribution margins ("mark-ups").

If it is difficult to carry out a market survey, or if few pork products are being sold in the country, it would be prudent to set prices on the basis of estimated unit production costs and an acceptable return on investment. It should be borne in mind that steps might have to be taken later, once manufacture has begun, to correct any resulting shortages or surpluses. For example, if shortages of a particular product developed, it might be possible to increase production or raise prices. On the other hand, surpluses might be exported or production reduced and other pork products manufactured instead. Ultimately, prices might have to be reduced in order to avoid higher losses.

IV.3 Siting of the plant

The location of the plant site should affect a project's profitability in terms of both fixed and variable costs. There are basically two options: to site the plant near the slaughterhouse or near the main area of consumption, assuming that these are some distance apart. The handling and transport costs of raw meat will be lower for the first option, but distribution costs for the products will be higher. The opposite conditions will apply if the plant is to be located near the main area of consumption. Furthermore, the price of land may differ from one area to another. Entrepreneurs should therefore carefully assess the effects on both investment costs and operating costs of alternative plant sites, with a view to identifying the least-cost option.

IV.4 Integration of manufacture of pork products
with other operations

As already indicated in Chapter I, a pork processing plant may be operated as a separate enterprise or may be attached to a slaughterhouse or a butchery business. In the latter two cases, the evaluation of the meat processing project may be carried out through what is called a "marginal" analysis. In this case, additional fixed and variable costs are compared to additional revenues, taking into consideration available facilities for the slaughterhouse or butchery and current sales from these businesses.

There may be certain advantages to be gained by integrating a pork processing plant into an existing slaughterhouse complex or butchery business rather than building a separate plant. For example, there might already be sufficient land available for a plant site at no additional cost, or existing buildings might be adapted at a relatively low cost. Transport facilities could also be used more effectively in the servicing of the slaughterhouse and processing plant.

A small plant attached to a butchery business may also improve the profitability of the latter. Excess supplies of fresh meat may be processed instead of being kept frozen or sold at low prices. Hired labour may be used in the meat processing unit during idle times. The only investment costs will in this case be limited to the acquisition of a few pieces of equipment and the expansion of existing buildings.

There are also various advantages derived from the setting up of a separate pork processing plant, including those derived from economies of scale. Thus, would-be meat processors are advised to carefully analyse the advantages and disadvantages of alternative options if funding is available for all of these. The evaluation framework described in this chapter could be used for the identification of the most profitable option.

Table V.1
Discount factor (F)

Year	Interest rate (percentage)																	
	5	6	8	10	12	14	15	16	18	20	22	24	25	26	28	30	35	40
1	0.952	0.943	0.926	0.909	0.893	0.877	0.870	0.862	0.847	0.833	0.820	0.806	0.800	0.794	0.781	0.769	0.741	0.714
2	1.859	1.833	1.783	1.736	1.690	1.647	1.626	1.605	1.566	1.528	1.492	1.457	1.440	1.424	1.392	1.361	1.289	1.224
3	2.723	2.673	2.577	2.487	2.402	2.322	2.283	2.246	2.174	2.106	2.042	1.981	1.952	1.923	1.868	1.816	1.696	1.589
4	3.546	3.465	3.312	3.170	3.037	2.914	2.855	2.798	2.690	2.589	2.494	2.404	2.362	2.320	2.241	2.166	1.997	1.849
5	4.330	4.212	3.993	3.791	3.605	3.433	3.352	3.274	3.127	2.991	2.864	2.745	2.689	2.635	2.532	2.436	2.220	2.035
6	5.076	4.917	4.623	4.355	4.111	3.889	3.784	3.685	3.498	3.326	3.167	3.020	2.951	2.885	2.759	2.643	2.385	2.168
7	5.786	5.582	5.206	4.868	4.564	4.288	4.160	4.039	3.812	3.605	3.416	3.242	3.161	3.003	2.937	2.802	2.508	2.263
8	6.463	6.210	5.747	5.335	4.968	4.639	4.487	4.344	4.078	3.837	3.619	3.421	3.329	3.241	3.076	2.925	2.598	2.331
9	7.108	6.802	6.247	5.759	5.328	4.946	4.772	4.607	4.303	4.031	3.786	3.566	3.463	3.366	3.184	3.019	2.665	2.379
10	7.722	7.360	6.710	6.145	5.650	5.216	5.019	4.833	4.494	4.192	3.923	3.682	3.571	3.465	3.269	3.092	2.715	2.414
11	8.306	7.887	7.139	6.495	5.938	5.453	5.234	5.029	4.656	4.327	4.035	3.776	3.656	3.544	3.335	3.147	2.752	2.438
12	8.863	8.384	7.536	6.814	6.194	5.660	5.421	5.197	4.793	4.439	4.127	3.851	3.725	3.606	3.387	3.190	2.779	2.456
13	9.394	8.853	7.904	7.103	6.424	5.842	5.583	5.342	4.910	4.533	4.203	3.912	3.780	3.656	3.427	3.223	2.799	2.468
14	9.899	9.295	8.244	7.367	6.628	6.002	5.724	5.468	5.008	4.611	4.265	3.962	3.824	3.695	3.459	3.249	2.814	2.477
15	10.380	9.712	8.559	7.606	6.811	6.142	5.847	5.575	5.092	4.675	4.315	4.001	3.859	3.726	3.483	3.268	2.825	2.484
16	10.838	10.106	8.851	7.824	6.974	6.265	5.954	5.669	5.162	4.730	4.357	4.033	3.887	3.751	3.503	3.283	2.834	2.489
17	11.274	10.477	9.122	8.022	7.120	6.373	6.047	5.749	5.222	4.775	4.391	4.059	3.910	3.771	3.510	3.295	2.840	2.492
18	11.690	10.828	9.372	8.201	7.250	6.467	6.128	5.818	5.273	4.812	4.419	4.080	3.928	3.786	3.529	3.304	2.844	2.494
19	12.085	11.158	9.604	8.365	7.366	6.550	6.198	5.877	5.316	4.844	4.442	4.097	3.942	3.799	3.539	3.311	2.848	2.496
20	12.462	11.470	9.818	8.514	7.469	6.623	6.259	5.929	5.353	4.870	4.460	4.110	3.954	3.808	3.546	3.316	2.850	2.497
21	12.821	11.764	10.017	8.649	7.562	6.687	6.312	5.973	5.384	4.891	4.476	4.121	3.963	3.816	3.551	3.320	2.852	2.498
22	13.163	12.042	10.201	8.772	7.645	6.743	6.359	6.011	5.410	4.909	4.488	4.130	3.970	3.822	3.556	3.323	2.853	2.498
23	13.489	12.303	10.371	8.883	7.718	6.792	6.399	6.044	5.432	4.925	4.499	4.137	3.976	3.827	3.559	3.325	2.854	2.499
24	13.799	12.550	10.529	8.985	7.784	6.835	6.434	6.073	5.451	4.937	4.507	4.143	3.981	3.831	3.562	3.327	2.855	2.499
25	14.094	12.783	10.675	9.077	7.843	6.873	6.464	6.097	5.467	4.948	4.514	4.147	3.985	3.834	3.564	3.329	2.856	2.499

CHAPTER VI

SOCIO-ECONOMIC AND ENVIRONMENTAL CONSIDERATIONS

The previous chapter was mostly of interest to established or potential meat processors since it dealt with the private profitability of pork processing units. This chapter reviews issues of interest to public planners and project evaluators from industrial development agencies, such as the employment effects of alternative meat processing technologies, foreign exchange expenditures, industrial location and the protection of the environment.

I. PROCESSED PIG-MEAT AND BASIC NEEDS

It is argued that the production of grain (e.g. maize) for the feeding of animals may not be justified in countries with a food shortage, since the nutritional value of a given quantity of grain is much higher than that of the equivalent amount of meat it helps produce. Thus, meat production in developing countries may only be justified under three main conditions: whenever there is a surplus of agricultural products; when pasture land is available which is not fit or required for the growing of food-grain; and when agricultural wastes are available. In many developing countries, one or more of the above conditions apply and meat is not, therefore, produced at the expense of the nutritional needs of low-income groups. This is particularly true in the case of pig-meat since hogs are often fed various agricultural by-products which would otherwise be wasted or transformed into fertilisers.

Whenever the production of fresh meat is justified from a socio-economic point of view, meat processing will also be justified for the following reasons. Firstly, a demand for various varieties of processed pig-meat will always exist in a country where the consumption of pork is allowed. This demand may be either satisfied through imports or through local production.

Obviously, the latter solution should be preferred since scarce foreign exchange will not be used for the import of processed pig-meat. Furthermore, low-income groups will not generally be able to afford expensive imports. Secondly, the production and/or marketing of fresh meat may not be possible in some areas of a country if transport in refrigerated vans is not available. Thus these areas may be supplied with processed pork products which will not spoil if kept at ambient temperatures, for a few days or weeks. Finally, there are cases where pig-meat trimmings or excess supplies of meat could be wasted if they are not processed. Altogether, the promotion of meat processing could help satisfy the basic need for food of low-income groups. There is, however, a danger that the price of fresh pig-meat may increase if too much of the available supply is diverted to the production of high-priced pork products which cannot be afforded by low-income groups.

II. THE EMPLOYMENT EFFECT OF ALTERNATIVE MEAT PROCESSING TECHNOLOGIES

The generation of productive employment is one of the major development objectives of developing countries. Technologies which may help to achieve this objective should therefore be favoured as long as labour is used in an efficient manner. In the case of pig-meat processing, the employment effect of alternative processing technologies may be analysed in relation to a hypothetical national production of 6,400 tonnes per annum of a variety of pork products. Production may be carried out in a number of small-scale plants (e.g. with a capacity of 80 tonnes to 100 tonnes per year) or in a large scale plant producing 6,400 tonnes per year (i.e. the whole national production).

Table VI.1 provides estimates of employment generated by the small-scale plants and the large-scale plant for the selected hypothetical yearly output. This table shows that the small-scale plants generate between 32 per cent and 47 per cent more labour per 1,000 tonnes of output than the large-scale plant. While the labour-intensity of the small-scale plants is substantially higher than that of the large-scale plant, the additional employment which may be generated in an average-sized developing country through the establishment of small-scale meat processing plants in place of large-scale units should be relatively small in view of the limited volume of fresh meat processed each year. On the other hand, the fact that small-scale plants will not need foreign expertise for their operation should be of particular interest to developing countries.

Table V.1

Employment generated by small-
and large-scale pig-meat processing plants

Plant size (tonnes/year)	No. of plants required to produce 6,400 tonnes	Employees per plant	Total employment	Man-years per 1,000 tonnes
80	80	8	640	100
100	64	9	576	90
6,400	1	435	435	68

III. INVESTMENT COSTS AND FOREIGN EXCHANGE EXPENDITURES

Projects which require relatively low capital and foreign exchange expenditures should be preferred by developing countries which suffer from shortages of investment funds and foreign exchange for the financing of development projects. If the above criterion is to be used for the selection of pig-meat processing technology, small-scale plants will be by far preferred, as indicated in Table V.2. This table shows that total investment costs per tonne of product for small-scale plants is approximately half of that needed for the large-scale plant. The same applies to foreign exchange costs.

In addition to making a better use of scarce investment and foreign exchange resources, small-scale pig-meat processing units may be established without government financial assistance or the need for foreign investments (e.g. in the form of outright ownership or joint ventures). Furthermore, small units may be established all over the country while large units must be established in the main urban areas since they usually require a fairly well-developed infrastructure. Thus, the adoption of small-scale technologies should allow a more balanced geographical development. This matter is further considered below.

Table V.2

Investment costs and foreign exchange expenditures

for small- and large-scale pork processing plant

Item	Plant size (tonnes/year)		
	80	100	6,400
Investment cost per plant (US$)	208 050	211 120	30 240 000
Foreign exchange cost per plant ($)	147 100	148 570	24 192 000
No. of plants required to produce 6,400 tonnes	80	64	1
Total investment cost (US$)	16 644 000	13 511 680	30 240 000
Investment cost per tonne of product (US$)	2 600	2 111	4 725
Total foreign exchange cost (US$)	11 768 000	9 508 450	24 192 000
Foreign exchange cost per tonne of output (US$)	1,839	1,470	3,780

[1] Investment cost per plant includes the cost of land, buildings and equipment.

[2] Foreign exchange cost per plant is assumed to be equal to the cost of equipment since, in most developing countries, the equipment must be imported. These estimates should be adjusted for countries which may produce some of the equipment.

IV. LOCATION OF PIG-MEAT PROCESSING PLANTS

The location of any industry may be a function of the following:

- transport costs of inputs and outputs and the availability of transport facilities;
- the availability of qualified manpower;
- the availability of regular supplies of water and energy; and

- government plans regarding the development of various areas of a country.

The last factor may induce governments to invest in infrastructural works or to provide various incentives in order to attract industries in particular areas of the country.

In the case of pig-meat processing, most of the above factors apply to a much lesser degree to small-scale units than to large-scale plants. The availability of good transport facilities is not essential if live or slaughtered hogs are available locally, since the output of a small-scale plant can be marketed locally. Thus the need for good roads or refrigerated trucks is much reduced.

The equipment used in small-scale plants is fairly simple and does not need highly qualified manpower. Small plants need only a qualified butcher with some management training. On the other hand, large-scale plants need highly qualified technicians who may not be available in small towns or rural areas.

The availability of regular supplies of water and energy applies equally to small- and large-scale plants. However, the requirement of these for the latter plants is much more important and any disruption in the supply of water or electricity could adversely affect plant profitability. On the other hand, a small-scale plant may adjust to such disruptions by storing water in a small tank or by using a small generator. Furthermore, losses incurred by a small-scale unit as a result of disruptions in water or electricity supply are much less serious than in the case of a large-scale plant.

In summary, governments wishing to create industries in backward areas of the country should find it much easier to establish small-scale pig-meat processing plants than large-scale plants in these areas. The establishment of large meat processing units in small towns or rural areas will require important infrastructural works which may not always be justified.

V. ENVIRONMENTAL EFFECTS OF ALTERNATIVE MEAT PROCESSING TECHNOLOGIES

In general, the environmental effects of food processing technologies is much more important in the case of large-scale than small-scale production.

Although the amount of pollutants per unit of output may be the same for all scales of production, the pollution generated by a large-scale plant in a given location could have more harmful effects than equivalent pollution generated by a number of small-scale plants located in various areas of a country.

However, the above general statement does not always apply. For example, a large-scale plant located in an urban area may be forced to implement various measures in order to minimize or eliminate the amount of pollution generated since the latter may not be tolerated by the urban population. On the other hand, a small-scale plant located in a rural area or small town may not be forced to apply similar measures because the amount of pollutants is tolerable.

The various effects of meat processing technologies on the environment are reviewed below, and remedial measures for the elimination or minimisation of these effects are described.

V.1 Waste disposal

The type and quantity of wastes resulting from meat processing will depend on whether the processing unit is operated as a separate business or is attached to a slaughterhouse. In the former case, the main waste materials include bones, some inedible trimmings and small amounts of grease and blood which may be contained in water used for cleaning the equipment, workbenches, etc. In the latter case, other waste materials must be disposed of, including blood, the content of edible offal (these are usually processed in a separate tripery), inedible offal, etc. In both cases, measures must be taken in order to dispose of these wastes in the most hygienic manner and to avoid the contamination of water sources or the spreading of diseases. Disposal of the most important waste materials is briefly described below.

Blood

Blood coagulates into a solid mass soon after leaving the body of the animal. It should not, therefore, be diverted into a sewage system unless the latter carries a sufficient volume of water to dilute the blood. The same applies to septic tanks. If blood from a slaughterhouse cannot be diverted to a main sewage system, and if no facilities are available to transform it into, for example, stock feed, it should be removed by special drains which have no connection with the sewer system. Blood may be disposed of by collecting it outside the slaughterhouse into a covered pit and letting it seep into the ground. The pit should be covered in order to avoid smells and insects. The special drain should be regularly flushed with water in order to avoid clogging of the system.

If the number of slaughtered animals is sufficiently large, it may be profitable to install a blood-processing unit for the production of stock-feed. In some countries, blood may also be processed for human consumption.

Bones

Meat processing plants generate large amounts of bones which must be disposed of. In many countries, bones are transformed into animal feed components or other industrial products. Bones may then be stored in sealed plastic bags outside the meat processing plant for periodic delivery to the bone processing plant.

Burning of wastes

Inedible offals and the content of edible ones (e.g. the stomach) should be collected into bins and disposed of by any acceptable method which does not harm the environment. In the case of small slaughterhouses, solid wastes may be burned in a simple incinerator made from an oil drum. Another alternative could be to dig a simple trench, fill it with branches and burn the wastes disposed over the branches. In general, the burying of solid wastes should be avoided since it is very likely that these will be dug up and eaten by scavengers. Burying may be used if holes are sufficiently deep and wastes are covered with lime. This method should also be used for the whole carcase of infected animals which are not fit for human consumption.

V.2 Final disposal of effluents

The final disposal of wastes in septic tanks, chemical precipitation or other costly methods can be avoided by proper screening of the effluents and by the removal of grease and particles suspended in the form of sludge (e.g. by use of a grease trap, of screens of galvanised wire over a gulley trap into which the drain discharges from the slaughterhouse). The final choice of effluent disposal must rest with the local authorities. There are, however, some basic principles which should be applied in the planning and design of slaughterhouses.

Effluents which are free from fat and other solid particles may be drained into shallow beds for seeping and evaporation. This method is not, however, recommended in warm climates because of the risk of mosquito breeding and the development of bad smells. Thus, evaporation beds should be used only in exceptional circumstances. Another simple method of sewage disposal consists in the use of one or a series of soakage pits. These should be 6 metres deep, with a diameter of 2 metres and should be covered in order to avoid bad smells. They work satisfactorily if used for small amounts of properly pre-treated effluents and if the type of soil is suitable. A third, cheap alternative is to divert effluents into long trenches (60 cm wide and 1.5 metres deep) filled with large stones to a depth of at least 60 cm from the top. It is advisable to lead the effluents first into a distribution box from which they can be diverted into lateral trenches for subsoil irrigation.

Whatever the system used, care should be taken to avoid contamination of water resources (e.g. aquifers, lakes) or to create new nuisances such as bad smells or the breeding of mosquitoes.

APPENDICES

APPENDIX I
Permitted levels of selected food additives

	Additive	Purpose	Product	Maximum permitted level
1.	Agar	Thickener	Cooked, cured ham	Limited by good manufacturing practice (GMP)
2.	BHA (Butylated Hydroxyanisole	Anti-oxidant	Dry sausage Fresh pork sausage	0.03 per cent of total weight, 0.01 per cent of fat content
3.	L-ascorbic acid, iso-ascorbic acid and sodium salts	Colour enhancer	Cooked, cured ham Cooked, cured, chopped meat	500 mg/kg (expressed as ascorbic acid)
4.	Natural flavourings as defined in the Codex Alimentarius	Flavour enhancer	Cooked, cured ham Cooked, cured chopped meat	Limited by GMP
5.	Natural smoke solutions	Flavour enhancer	Cooked, cured meat	Limited by GMP
6.	Sodium citrate	Colour enhancer	Cooked, cured ham Cooked, cured, chopped meat	Limited by GMP
7.	Disodium 5-Guanylate	Flavour enhancer	Cooked, cured ham Cooked, cured, chopped meat	500 mg/kg (expressed as Guanylic Acid)
8.	Disodium 5-Inosinate	Flavour enhancer	Cooked, cured ham Cooked, cured, chopped meat	500 mg/kg (expressed as Inosinic Acid)
9.	Monosodium Glutamate	Flavour enhancer	Cooked, cured ham Cured, chopped meat	2,000 mg/kg (expressed as Glutamic Acid) 5,000 mg/kg /(expressed as Glutamic Acid)
10.	Sodium nitrate Potassium Nitrate	Preservative	Cooked, cured ham	500 mg/kg (expressed as Sodium Nitrate)
11.	Sodium nitrite Potassium nitrite	To fix colour	Cooked, cured ham Cured products	125 mg/kg (expressed Sodium Nitrite)
12.	Sodium and potassium phosphates	Binders	Ham and cured products	3,000 mg/kg (expressed as P_2O_5)
13.	Glucono-Delta-Lactone	To accelerate colour fixing	Cooked, cured, chopped meat	3,000 mg/kg
14.	Edible gelatine	Thickener	Ham	Limited by GMP

APPENDIX II

Factors used in the estimation of meat products occupancy in meat curing and maturation rooms[1]

Commodity	Processing	Container	Kg product per m^3
Fresh sausage	Holding prior to despatch	Aluminium stacked boxes, 0.3 m^3	600
Tea sausage	Minced pork (5°C to 8°C)	Polypropylene stacked boxes, 0.25 m^3	500
		Aluminium stacked boxes, 0.3 m^3	600
	Maturation (20°C to 22°C)	Sausage pole, static	60
		Sausage pole, mobile pallet, 1.8 m high	50
Mortadella	Emulsion trays (2°C)	Aluminium stacked boxes, 0.3m^3	800
	Dehydration (10°C)	Sausage pole, static	90
Frankfurters	Chilling after cooking	Sausage pole	65
Cooked ham	Curing in brine	Mobile curing bin 300 1 (legs)	180
		Aluminium stacked boxes, 0.3 m^3 (shoulders)	120
	Maturation	Maturation racks (legs shoulders, "bone-in")	350
	Cooking mould	Ham mould	500

[1]These factors are included for information only and refer to Models 1 and 2. They are estimations of product occupancies and refer to the meat or meat product (i.e. they contain allowances for brine, etc.), but do not include allowance for movement. In the case of small, multiple occupancy cold stores, the movement allowance factors are 1.2 for area and 1.4 for height. .

APPENDIX III

Factors used for the estimation of equipment
and labour requirements

These factors are included for information only and refer to Models 1 and 2. They are estimations of average production rates.

Operation	Rate
Primal butchery rate	330 kg/hour
Deboning	
Debone to hand mincer	45 kg/hour
Debone to power mincer (100 kg/hr)	66 kg/hour
Debone to power mincer (200 kg/hr)	75 kg/hour
Mincing	
Hand mincing	50 kg/hour
Power mincing	100 kg/hour
High power mincing	>200 kg/hour
(rate is function of capacity)	
Mixing	
Hand mixing of 2.5 kg batches	5 minutes
Power mixing of 5.0 kg batches	8 minutes
Power mixing of 10.0 kg batches	12 minutes
Power mixing of 20.0 kg batches	15 minutes
Stuffing	
Hand stuffing	60 kg/hour
Hydraulic stuffing	150 kg/hour
Linking	
Hand only	50 kg/hour
Packing	
Simple	40 kg/hour
Assisted table	80 kg/hour

EQUIPMENT REQUIREMENTS FOR MODEL 1 AND 2

Item	Life (years)	Capacity per unit	Rating[1] (kw per unit)	Model 1		Model 2	
				Number	Use per 8 hours[1] (per cent)	Number	Use per 8 hours[1] (per cent)
Butchery and sausage processing area							
Meat cutting table	10			3		4	
Preparation table	10			2		1	
Platform scale	15	100 kg		1		1	
Mincer	10	100 kg/hour	0.75	1	45	1	25
Mixer	10	30 litres[2]	0.6[2]	1	40	1	15
15							
Sink unit	10			1		1	
Immersion heater	10		1.5	1	50	1	50
Whetstone knife sharpener	5		0.1	1	5	1	5
Scale	15			1		1	
Processing hall							
Meat cutting table	10			2		3	
Preparation table	10			1		1	
Brine injection pump	10	300 litres/hour	0.5	1	10	1	10
Balance	15	10 kg	0.01	1	100	1	100
Meat tumbler	10	30 litres	0.5	–		1	40
Flace ice maker	10	100 kg/day	0.5	1	225	–	
Bowl chopper	10	30 litres	3.5	1	40	–	
Hydraulic sausage filler	10	25 kg		1	50	–	
Sausage clipper unit	5			1		–	
Refrigerator	10	0.5 m³	0.15	1	225	1	225
Metal bins (seamless)	10	300 litres		15		25	
Metal bins (seamless)	10			15		15	
Dry goods store							
Pan scales	15			1		1	
Preparation tables	10			2		2	
Ingredients bins	10			15		15	
Cooking/smoking rooms							
Smoking/cooking/drying cabinet	15		8	1	150	1	100
Smoke generator	10			1		1	
Smoke trolley	5			2		2	
Ham cooking kettles	15	8 hams[3]	10[3]	2	100	3	100
Preparation tables	15			1		1	
Refrigeration units							
Fresh meat room (0°C)	5	15.5 m³	3.5	1	225	1	225
Curing room (0°C)	5	15.5 m³	3.5	1	225	1	225
Ham maturation room (0°C)	5	15.5 m³	3.5	1	225	1	225
Finished product store, divied (0°C)	5	10.0 m³	3.0[4]	1	225	1	225
Packaging room							
Meat wrapping table	10			1		1	
Assorted trays	15			1		1	
Scale	15			1	50	1	50
Miscellaneous							
High pressure washer	15		2.2	1	20	1	20
Electrocutor	10		0.05	2	300	2	300
Platform scales	15	250 kg		1		1	
Chlorination unit	15			1		1	
Office furniture	15						
Fans	5		0.1	2	100	2	100

[1] Estimation of electricity consumption. Figures shown in the table for rating (kW) and percentage use of equipment per 8 hours are used to calculate cost of electricity consumption in the two cases illustrated in Chapter V. Some items are used for more than 8 hours per 24 hours day and the percentage figure is therefore over 100. For example, refrigeration equipment is in use 24 hours per day and actually consumes electricity for about 3/4 of this time, hence the figure of 225 per cent per 8 hours shown in the table. Refrigeration equipment is assumed to be in use 7 days per week.

[2] Finished product store in Model 2 is 15.5 m³. Rating is 3.5 kW (for comminuted ham).

[3] Ham cooking kettles in Model 2 have a capacity of 12 hams each. Rating is 15 kW per unit.

[4] Mixer capacity in Model 2 is 10 litres. Rating is 0.5 kW.

APPENDIX V

INFORMATION SOURCES

SELECTED DIRECTORIES

The Almanac of the Canning, Freezing, Preserving Industries
Annual
Publisher: E.E. Judge and Sons,

        P.O. Box 866

        Westminster, Maryland 21157, United States

Food Processing Catalogue: Ingredients, Equipment and Supplies
Bi-yearly
Publisher: Putnam Publishing Co.

        11 East Delaware Place,

        Chicago, Illinois 60611, United States

SELECTED CURRENT PERIODICALS

Meat Plant Magazine
Monthly
Publisher: Albert Todoroff,

        10225 Bach Boulevard,

        St. Louis, Missouri 63132, United States

Meat Processing
Monthly
Publisher: Davis Publishing Co.

        645 North Michigan Avenue

        Chicago, Illinois 60611, United States

Food Technology
Monthly
Publisher: Institute of Food Technologists

        221 North Lasalle Street,

        Chicago, Illinois 60601, United States

Journal of Food Science and Technology

Quarterly

Publisher: Association of Food Technologists (India)
         Central Food Technological Research Institute
         Mysore 2, India

Journal of Food Technology

Quarterly

Publisher: Blackwell Scientific Publications
         Osney Mead,
         Oxford OX2 OEL, United Kingdom.

BIBLIOGRAPHY

Ashbrook, F.G.: <u>Butchering, processing and preservation of meat</u> (New York, van Nostrand, 1955).

Brandly, P.J. et al. : <u>Meat hygiene</u> (Philadelphia, Lea and Febiger, 1966).

Carosella, M.; Johnston W.R.;. Surkiewicz, F.B.: "Bacteriological survey of frankfurters produced at establishment under federal inspection" in <u>Journal of Food Technology</u> (Oxford), Vol. 39, No. 1, 1976.

Food and Agriculture Organisation of the United Nations: <u>Trade Yearbook</u>, (Rome) various issues 1967, 1970, 1973, 1976, 1979.

_____: <u>Animal by-products: Processing and utilisation</u> (Rome, 1978).

_____: <u>Guide to the safe use of food additives</u> (Rome, 1979).

_____: <u>Food preservation: Fish, meat equipment</u>, Economic and Social Development Series No. 5/1 (Rome, 1979).

_____: <u>Meat handling in under-developed countries: Slaughter and preservation</u> (Rome, 1963).

Furia, T.: <u>Handbook of food additives</u>, (Cleveland, Ohio, CRC Press, 2nd ed., 1975).

Gerrard, F.: <u>Sausage and small goods production</u> (London, Hill, 1969).

_____: <u>Meat technology</u> (London, Hill, 1971).

Jay, J.M.; Shelef, L.A.: "Microbial modifications in raw and processed meats and poultry at low temperatures", in <u>Journal of Food Technology</u>, Vol. 32, No. 5, 1978.

Jones, H.R.: <u>Pollution control in meat, poultry and seafood processing</u> (Park Ridge, Noyes Data Corporation, 1974).

Karmas, E.: <u>Fresh meat processing</u> (Park Ridge, Noyes Data Corporation, 1970).

_____: Meat product manufacture (Park Ridge, Noyes Data Corporation, 1970).

Price, J.F.: The science of meat and meat products (San Francisco, California, W. Freeman, 1972).

Rack, G.B.; Rinsted, R.: Hygiene in food manufacturing and handling (London, Food Trade Press, 1973).

United Nations Industrial Development Organisation: Information sources on the meat processing industry (New York, United Nations, 1976).

QUESTIONNAIRE

1. Full name...

2. Address..
   ....
   ....

3. Profession (check the appropriate case)

   Established meat processor................................/__/
   If yes, indicate scale of production.............................

   Government official......................................./__/
   If yes, specify position...

   Employee of a financial institution......................./__/
   If yes, specify position...

   University staff member.................................../__/

   Staff member of a technology institution................../__/
   If yes, indicate name of institution.............................
   ....

   Staff member of a training institution..................../__/
   If yes, specify..
   ....

   Other, specify...
   ....

4. From where did you get a copy of this memorandum?
   Specify if obtained free or bought...............................
   ....

5. Did the memorandum help you achieve the following:
   (Check the appropriate case)

   Learn about meat processing techniques you were not aware of   /__/

   Estimate unit production costs for various scales
   of production/technologies   /__/

   Order equipment for local manufacture   /__/

   Improve your current production technique   /__/

   Cut down operating costs   /__/

   Improve the quality of meat products   /__/

   Decide which scale of production/technology to
   adopt for a new meat processing plant   /__/

   If a Government employee, to formulate new measures
   and policies for the meat processing industry   /__/

   If an employee of a financial institution, to assess
   a request of a loan for the establishment of a meat
   processing plant   /__/

   If a trainer in a training institution, to use the
   memorandum as supplementary training material   /__/

   If an international expert, to better advise counter-
   parts on meat processing technologies   /__/

6. Is the memorandum detailed enough in terms of: Yes   No

   - Description of technical aspects........................____....._____

- Costing information......................................____······____

- Information on socio-economic impact...................____······____

- Bibliographical information............................____······____

If some of the answers are 'No', please indicate why below or on a separate sheet:

....
....
....

7. How may this memorandum be improved if a second edition is to be published?...
....
....

8. Please send this questionnaire, duly completed to:

       Technology and Employment Branch
       International Labour Office
       CH-1211 GENEVA 22 (Switzerland)

9. In case you need additional information on some of the issues covered by this memorandum, the ILO will do its best to provide the requested information.

www.ingramcontent.com/pod-product-compliance
Lightning Source LLC
Chambersburg PA
CBHW082302210326
41519CB00062B/6957